I (

Bible

AND I'M

Not Afraid

TO USE IT

AN OPERATING GUIDE FOR LIFE

Laura Stierman

Foreword by Melanie Hart

theWORD among us® press

Published by The Word Among Us Press
7115 Guilford Drive, Suite 100
Frederick, Maryland 21704

wau.org

25 24 23 22 21   1 2 3 4 5

ISBN: 978-1-59325-520-6
eISBN: 978-1-59325-521-3

Design by Suzanne Earl

Made and printed in the United States of America

Library of Congress Control Number: 2020925422

Contents

FOREWORD

Do you ever feel like your spiritual and emotional well has just run dry? Perhaps it's even a daily occurrence—the result of a life lived for everyone *else*. Maybe your well has been emptied while changing diapers or journeying with teens through emotional drama. Or while navigating a rigorous work schedule or financial or health or pandemic stresses. Perhaps the dryness you feel is the result of worrying about adult children and their spiritual lives.

It's been said that the Lord entrusts his greatest battles to his strongest warriors, but more often than not, after a day of playing chauffeur and cleaning lady, cook and counselor, wife and tutor, I sometimes worry the Lord thinks too much of me! Seldom is the night when I have one neuron still firing that I reach for my Bible looking for solace or answers to my life's greatest struggles. Opening the pages of Scripture can feel almost overwhelming for these tired eyes, and yet I somehow find the time to scroll through my social media feed.

Growing up a Protestant girl in the South, I often saw my grandmothers and great grandmothers clutching the word of God and reading it aloud. Their Bibles were revered, worn from overuse and always within arms' reach. "They were so holy," I sometimes think to myself, celebrating their memories whilst lamenting my lack of spiritual discipline.

When I became Catholic as a child and took ownership of my faith in high school and college, I grew in my admiration of God's word but was never really given a strong foundation or a "rhythm" with which to pray it. I desired to read the Bible, but I lacked the tools to figure out how to start and where to go. Most Bible studies I came across seemed more concerned with *information* than *inspiration*. As a woman, I longed for something deeper, something that would help me ponder God's word like the Virgin Mary:

> Mary kept all these things, pondering them in her heart. (Luke 2:19)

What I would give to have more time to reflect, to pray, and to read in the midst of my days' busyness and my weeks' stresses!

In *Three to Get Married*, Venerable Fulton Sheen discusses both the complementarity and uniqueness of men and women. He notes the difference in the way we were created—man from dust and woman from rib:

> Man lives more in the external world, because from
> the earth ... Woman lives more in the internal world,
> because she was created from an inner, human life.
> Man is more interested in the outer world, woman
> in the inner world. Man talks about things, woman
> more about persons.[1]

That simple insight has always spoken to my female heart. As women, we are *created* differently. Our collective desire as women is for deeper human and emotional connection.

One of the reasons I genuinely enjoyed the book you are holding is that it drew me into a deeper connection with the Lord through each woman's story. Laura breathes new insights into passages I've heard a dozen times, and she brings them to life in such personal ways. Coming face-to-face with these women in Scripture, I kept finding bits of myself. Whether discussing Martha or Mary Magdalene or even the woman caught in adultery, their interactions with the Lord spoke truth into my life.

As I read this book, I found myself laughing, nodding, even tearing up at the reminders of God's great love for me not just as wife or mother or "doer" but as his daughter. With every turn of the page, it is evident that Laura is both a true scholar and a deeply spiritual woman. She skillfully unpacks the mystery of the feminine genius with keen insight, connecting the proverbial dots between Scripture, Church teachings, and everyday life issues. Though deep, it's not too heavy to move through at the end of a long day as you collapse onto the couch or curl up in a cozy bed.

This little gem makes the Bible both relatable and accessible for modern daughters of God, and I, for one, am looking forward to sharing it with the women in my life. We all need the Lord, but we also need our sisters in Christ to journey beside us, comfort us and challenge us to "ponder" things in our hearts daily.

In the busyness of life and trying to fill everyone else's wells, we might forget that we too need to be filled. I invite you to take a moment for yourself now. Close your eyes, take a deep breath, and invite the Holy Spirit in. The Lord desires to speak to your heart with every turn of the page of the book you are holding. Give yourself the gift of your time now, and let God's timeless word refill the well of your soul in a timely new way. Happy reading!

Melanie Hart

My Dear Sister in Christ,

Have you ever wondered if the Lord would speak to you? Or if you could be inspired or guided by the word of God? Or perhaps you attended Bible studies that left you disappointed or even hurt?

If any of these questions ring true in your heart, this book is for you.

This little operating guide is designed to help you deepen your relationship with the Lord through Scripture and apply his word to your life. It's an excursion with an open-ended destination, led by women whose stories have something to say to you.

Along the way, I hope you nod knowingly at times, stop reading for a second or two to process a sentence that touches your heart, and maybe get up mid-chapter to find a tissue. I hope you smile at parts, finding a freedom and comradery you didn't think possible. And even better, I hope you laugh out loud, as laughter heals the spirit and soothes the soul.

One last thing: write in your Bible. Highlight, underline, use exclamation points, and make notes in the margins! Let it become a familiar friend who knows your secrets and struggles as well as your strength, your courage, and your beauty inside and out.

Most of all, I hope that when you need wisdom and strength, you will grab your Bible, find a favorite passage, and listen for the Lord. Because you own a Bible, and you are *not* afraid to use it.

Laura

INTRODUCTION

For I know the plans I have for you,
says the LORD, plans for welfare and
not for evil, to give you a future and a
hope. (Jeremiah 29:11)

Have you ever played Bible roulette? You know, "Lord, I'm in some difficulty here, and I need some words of wisdom."

Perhaps you are waiting for Mr. Right, wondering if love will ever find you, since Mr. Wrong has come and gone again, leaving you with shattered dreams and a heart aching for companionship. You say to the Lord, "I know you have a plan for me and my beloved. I know you have set him apart just for me. Give me hope."

You grab your Bible, say a quick prayer, close your eyes, and *voilà*, 1 Corinthians 7:8: "To the unmarried and the widows I say that it is well for them to remain single as I do."

Decidedly unhelpful.

Or let's say you have a stubborn and slightly rebellious college-age son who won't listen to reason or to the wisdom you share with him. You grab your Bible, say a quick prayer, close your eyes, and *voilà*, Deuteronomy 21:18-21:

> If a man has a stubborn and rebellious son, who will not obey the voice of his father or the voice of his mother, and, though they chastise him, will not give heed to them, then his father and his mother shall take hold of him and bring him out to the elders of his city at the gate of the place where he lives, and they shall say to the elders of his city, "This our son is stubborn and rebellious, he will not obey our voice; he is a glutton and a drunkard." Then all the men of the city shall stone him to death with stones; so you shall purge the evil from your midst; and all Israel shall hear, and fear.

Again, decidedly unhelpful.

Or perhaps you are my soul sister in productivity. We fall into bed late at night and try to sleep, but the neurons firing in our brains have made a raging bonfire of things yet to do. We wonder if we have marshmallows in the pantry, where we hid the Hershey's, and if that s'more might be even better with a peanut butter cup tucked inside. Our minds are in a constant state of movement, even when our bodies are not. We are in desperate need of the Lord's stillness and peace.

So we grab the cellphone off the nightstand, open the Bible app, say a quick prayer, close our eyes, and *voilà*, Isaiah 48:22: "'There is no peace,' says the LORD, 'for the wicked.'"

Double sigh.

Are you with me here?

We might stop opening our Bibles because it isn't helpful. We stop trying to figure out what the Lord is saying to us because it isn't making sense. We lose faith in the Holy Spirit because, you know, it just doesn't seem to be working. We don't know the Lord's plans. We can't hear how his word is beneficial for us, and we don't hold much hope that our luck is going to change anytime soon in the game of Bible roulette.

I beg to differ.

You see, God does want to give you hope through his word. Our Lord does want you to encounter his voice through the Scriptures. God does want the Holy Spirit to stir your heart, mind, and soul. God does indeed have plans for your future and for your welfare.

How do I know that? Because I've had my heart broken into a thousand pieces, with fragments of shattered dreams piercing my soul; I've been the mom of a stubborn son; and I've glanced at a clock that reads 3:47 a.m. and been desperate for the brain bonfire to burn down.

Yet I have also encountered the Lord in Scripture. I've imagined him standing next to me as he did the woman at the well and healing me as he did Mary of Magdala. I have watched him obey his mother at the wedding at Cana, and I have seen the way he loved the sinner woman. I've befriended the Lord as did Martha, and I've abandoned him as did Peter. I've cried with him at the tomb of Lazarus and walked with him on the road to Emmaus.

The Lord has spoken to my heart in my longing and in my woundedness. He has helped me in my need and healed me in my brokenness. He has restored the dignity I had lost, the simple life I had abandoned, and the peace I had given away. He has loved me through my suffering. I have heard him whisper my name and call out my imperfections. He has made me a better woman—the woman I was meant to be, one with a future and a hope.

How did I go from being afraid to open my Bible to encountering the Lord in his word? It was simple, really. I learned how to combine Scripture with the imaginative practice of placing myself in the scene. Called the SOAP method, it is also used for a variety of things like emergency room triage, business acquisitions, and law procedures. It looks like this when applied to Scripture:

> S – Scripture: define the passage
> O – Observe: discover the message
> A – Application: apply what you learned
> P – Practical: take action

This SOAP method has become my operating guide for reading the Bible. It is simple, concise, and meaningful.

It has helped me navigate the Sacred Scriptures and deepen my relationship with Jesus Christ. Let's explore how this works.

Scripture: Define the Passage

First, create a space in your day and a place in your home for prayer. Choose a time that you're pretty sure you won't be interrupted. Then pick your sacred space. Perhaps it's a favorite rocking chair, a corner of your sofa, or your space at the kitchen table. Pick up your favorite Bible, and offer a simple prayer to the Holy Spirit, such as "Come Holy Spirit. Open my heart to see what you want me to see and to hear what you want me to hear through your words. Thank you for your presence as I read the word of God."

Next, select the passage you are going to read. You might want to look up the Sunday Gospel reading, a psalm you recently heard, or a parable. I strongly recommend that you read your chosen passage a second or even a third time. Look closely at what the text is saying. For example, you might notice that Eve didn't pluck an apple from the tree, and Mary Magdalene was not a prostitute. Or that the hemorrhaging woman had bled for twelve years and that the woman with the alabaster jar was watched by a room full of men. Sometimes you notice just a fun fact, as in the case of the apple, but sometimes you might learn something that changes the meaning of an entire story for you.

In the chapters that follow, I will take what I know about the women of this time period, the towns they live in, their roles in culture and religious life, and the consequences their actions might bear, and I will give them personality. Each chapter opens with this *imaginative* story of our heroine, although all but one are flesh-and-blood women who encountered the Lord in history. I will invite you to think about the woman, her circumstances, what she might be feeling, and how she thinks others see her. I encourage you to consider your own imaginings about people, settings, and stories.

Observe: Discover the Message

Read your chosen passage again, and observe how the words on the page strike you. What stands out as you read? The woman who dries the feet of Jesus with her hair: what is it about an uncovered head? The woman caught in adultery: where is her beloved while she is the victim of public shaming? Why does Mary of Magdala head to the tomb before sunrise; why is she not sleeping?

In looking closely at a story, you might hear the Lord whispering in your ear, telling you what you need to hear, and leading you deeper into a relationship with him.

If we want to learn from the men and women in our Bibles, it's helpful to know a little about the person telling the story, what he wants to tell us, and where we stand in his world. You can glean much information from the footnotes in your Bible. If your Bible has minimal footnotes, or if you want to delve more deeply into the context, you may want to pick up a Bible commentary.

*A*pplication: Apply What You Learned

Next it's time to look at your own life to ponder and pray. All the men and women we encounter in the Bible have something to say to us. The Lord does too. He wants to answer the desires of our hearts.

Here we ask questions and apply concepts based on the text. What is God saying to you about simplicity as Mary gives her *fiat*? How is he sharing in your grief as Mary Magdalene runs to Jesus' empty tomb? What does he say about your love through the sinful woman who anoints his feet? Why does he not answer the prayers of Elizabeth and Zechariah until they are old and gray—and what might that mean for you? Put yourself in the events that unfold. Make it personal.

*P*ractical: Take Action

Finally, think about how your reading, pondering, and applying might lead you toward an outward expression. "Doing something" is part of every operating guide. Concrete action—something practical that you will do—is integral to the faith life. We want to encounter our sisters and brothers in Scripture and let our newfound friend-ships change us.

You might spend an extra few minutes in prayer, sched-ule coffee with a friend who needs you, or focus on your family. Perhaps you will say no to things you don't want to do and yes to those you do without feeling guilty. In the pages that follow, I will offer one or two suggestions to put action to each Scripture story that we ponder.

This book is intended to help you deepen your relation-ship with the Lord through Scripture—a little operating guide to help you find your way. Throughout the next eight chapters, I hope you not only learn the value of a new method but also hear God's voice as you ponder the words of Scripture. The Lord desires that you live an abun-dant life, and he promises that when you seek him, you will find him (see John 10:10; Jeremiah 29:11-14). He has left his word to guide you along this journey. I pray that the time you spend reading his word using the SOAP method will help you grow closer to him and his amazing plan for your life. Grab your favorite Bible, and let's begin!

CHAPTER ONE

Mary, Mother of Jesus

"Let it be to me according to your word." (Luke 1:38, NABRE)

In the sixth month, the angel Gabriel was sent from God to a town of Galilee called Nazareth, to a virgin betrothed to a man named Joseph, of the house of David, and the virgin's name was Mary. And coming to her, he said, "Hail, favored one! The Lord is with you." But she was greatly troubled at what was said and pondered what sort of greeting this might be. Then the angel said to her, "Do not be afraid, Mary, for you have found favor with God. Behold, you will conceive in your womb and bear a son, and you shall name him Jesus. He will be great and will be called Son of the Most High, and the Lord God will give him the throne of David his father, and he will rule over the house of Jacob forever, and of his kingdom there will be no end." But Mary said to the angel, "How can this be, since I have no relations with a man?" And the angel said to her in reply, "The holy Spirit will come upon you, and the power of the Most High will overshadow you. Therefore the child to be born will be called holy, the Son of God. And behold, Elizabeth, your relative, has also conceived a son in her old age, and this is the sixth month for her who was called barren; for nothing will be impossible for God." Mary said, "Behold, I am the handmaid of the Lord. May it be done to me according to your word." Then the angel departed from her. (Luke 1:26-38, NABRE)

$\mathcal{S}$cripture: Define the Passage

Do you know this young girl named Mary? She is from the small town of Nazareth. Like all Jewish girls, she learns to keep house and pray *Shabbat* through the example of her mother. She learns the value of hard work and the importance of prayer through the example of her father. She knows the sounds of her father leaving for work, of her mother returning from market, and of the laughter of little ones greeting each other.

She knows sadness too. She hears the sound of grief as a child dies of fever or a mother gives her life for her newborn. She laments over a harvest destroyed by locusts and a season without rain.

There is fear in her world. She sees the wolves in the hills and a leper in the distance.

But there is faith in God that overcomes the grief and the fear. In the *Shabbat*, Mary learns the language of trust and the songs of awe. Her ancestors wandered for an entire generation before entering this land. The prophets Isaiah, Ezekiel, Amos, and Micah gave them hope for the future.

She knows the anointed one will come in God's time, and this gives her peace.

Her thoughts turn to Joseph. She hears her parents whispering about him when they think she is not listening. He is a good man, a faithful man. He is gentle and kind by all accounts, a *tekton* who is good with his hands and will build a life for them. She thinks he will make a good husband. At sixteen or so, she can think these things.

Still her mind wanders often to God. She feels a presence in the synagogue—one that, as she looks around at the other girls her age, she senses that she alone feels. She loves the unrolling of the scrolls and the recitation of their words. The poetry of the psalms is music to her ears. The rhythmic reading of the lyrical text stirs her soul. God whispers to her.

After the angel appeared, she realizes how simple it all was. There was no fanfare, no blowing of trumpets or asking permission of parents or parading through town to consult the rabbi. She wasn't asked to recite the *Shema* or some other verses from Sacred Scriptures to test her worthiness.

Of course, she had a question or two. She is an intelligent young woman, after all. But when the momentous question came, she was asked for a simple *yes* or *no*. *Will I*, or *won't I*?

Observe: Discover the Message

The Gentile convert and physician-turned-evangelist Luke wrote the good news of Jesus Christ sometime after AD 70, when the Roman army destroyed the Jewish Temple, but before AD 100, when John wrote his account. Most biblical scholars agree on an AD 80–90 composition date.

Luke wrote to a non-Jewish audience. He called upon Jesus' followers to care for the poor, the lowly, the outcast, the widows, the lepers, the homeless, and all those in need of the Divine Physician.

Although Luke wrote to Gentiles, his audience knew about Jewish family life. Generally speaking, Jewish life centered around the Friday *Shabbat* dinner; the *Tanakh* (Old Testament), read in the synagogues and filtered through the Sadducees and Pharisees; and an agrarian lifestyle. Hearth and home were the women's domain, while men practiced the trades. Girls learned from their mothers how to prepare meals, sew garments, clean house, and give birth. Boys learned from their fathers to tend sheep, grow crops, study *Torah*, and build furniture. Marriages were arranged by parents, and a young girl like Mary would have been engaged around the age of sixteen.

Luke opens his Gospel with two unlikely conceptions: that of John the Baptist (1:5-25) and that of Jesus of Nazareth (1:26-38). Neither was expected, although Elizabeth had been praying for a child.

The angel who appears to Mary and to her cousin's husband is Gabriel. His name means "God is my strength" or "mighty man of God." God is going to unleash a power into the world that has never been seen before. Perhaps both meanings of the word "Gabriel" converge here.

Maybe God means to bestow upon Mary the strength that she needs to carry the mighty man of God. Mary, after all, is a young girl in a small town, engaged to be married. She thinks she knows where her life is headed. It will be a simple and quiet life in Nazareth, where she will be surrounded by those who know and love her. If God is going to upend those plans, she's going to need strength.

> The angel Gabriel was sent from God . . . to a virgin.
> . . . And coming to her, he said, "Hail, favored one! The
> Lord is with you." (Luke 1:26-28, NABRE)

Gabriel's first words to Mary are meant to both single her out and get her attention: "Hail, favored one! The Lord is with you." The root word in Greek that the angel uses for "favored" is *charis*, meaning "pleasing, generous, kindly, gentle, thankful"—"graced," we say. Gabriel then tells us that the Lord is "with" Mary, meaning "together with," "on the same side as," or "among." Mary is both faith-filled and faithful. Her inner disposition is reflected by her outward actions. She is a singular young woman, a beloved daughter. There is no duplicity in her.

But she was greatly troubled at what was said and pondered what sort of greeting this might be. (Luke 1:29, NABRE)

Mary does not understand Gabriel's greeting. She is confused (*diatarasso*) and "greatly troubled" at first. She is afraid, as Gabriel knows. It seems as though, in her humility, she believes she is no different from any other Jewish girl. Perplexed that she is singled out, she ponders what this means.

Mary engages her intellect. She ponders (*dialogizomai*). She may not understand why she is favored, yet she is open to God's thoughts of her. She does not reject the compliment! She does not run or hide from God's vision of who she is.

The angel said to her, "Do not be afraid, Mary, for you have found favor with God." (Luke 1:30, NABRE)

The angel Gabriel speaks to Mary's fear and responds before she can utter a word. Although it is the angel speaking, God is the one at work.

Angels have no capacity for learned experience; they are simply God's messengers. Indeed, the Greek word for "messenger" is *angelos*. It is God who knows Mary's fear and asks her to leave it behind: "Do not be afraid, Mary, for you have found favor with God." Again, she is reminded of her identity as a beloved daughter.

> "Behold, you will conceive in your womb and bear
> a son, and you shall name him Jesus. He will be
> great and will be called Son of the Most High, and
> the Lord God will give him the throne of David his
> father, and he will rule over the house of Jacob
> forever, and of his kingdom there will be no end."
> (Luke 1:31-33, NABRE)

Gabriel gets right to the point. It's a simple proposition: Mary will conceive Jesus by the power of the Holy Spirit, and Jesus will rule over the house of Jacob forever. Indeed, his kingdom will have no boundaries.

> "How can this be, since I have no relations with a
> man?" (Luke 1:34, NABRE)

Mary, speaking for the first time, asks only one question: "How can this be?" Notice that she has left fear behind; this is an immediate response to Gabriel's command, "Do not be afraid" (Luke 1:30, NABRE). She is moving forward and is open to the life God has for her.

Hers is a reasonable question, a most important one. Do you also notice the things she does *not* ask? She does not question her value in the eyes of God. She does not ask if her life will be easy or if she will suffer. She does not question the future; she only ponders the present.

> The angel said to her in reply, "The holy Spirit will
> come upon you, and the power of the Most High will

overshadow you. Therefore the child to be born will be called holy, the Son of God. And behold, Elizabeth, your relative, has also conceived a son in her old age, and this is the sixth month for her who was called barren; for nothing will be impossible for God." (Luke 1:35-37, NABRE)

Gabriel responds with three statements: the Holy Spirit will come upon you and the Most High overshadow you; the child will be called the Son of God; and by the way, your elderly cousin Elizabeth is with child, for nothing is impossible for God.

Mary responds, "Behold, I am the handmaid of the Lord. May it be done to me according to your word" (Luke 1:38, NABRE).

A simple yes.

*A*pplication: Apply What You Learned

Gabriel asks Mary a question, and the simple way in which she responds can be the guide for all the decisions we make.

Will I, or *won't I*?

We all desire this thing called simplicity. "I desire a complicated life," said no one ever. And yet our lives tend toward messiness. There are playdates and parties to arrange. We have soccer and school carpools to manage. We sit with executives in boardrooms and two-year-olds in bathrooms. We think about dinner before breakfast and the gym at the end of a long day. We sort clothes to send to international missions and deliver canned goods to our local food shelves.

We sometimes forget to eat but remember the lunch that needs to get to school. We pray for peace in the car on the way to work and wisdom on the way home. We have phones that we think make our lives easier, but rarely do we actually talk to someone. And we have social media to complicate matters, but we will return to that later.

Nothing is ever a simple yes or no with us.

In his *Letter to Women*, St. John Paul II writes of a woman's ability to see things holistically. Ordinary women have an innate capacity to "acknowledge the person, because they see persons with their hearts."[2] Thus we are able to challenge the status quo and change the world and solve all kinds of problems, including "leisure time, the quality of life, . . . euthanasia, drugs, health care."[3] Yes, he said that. It's a letter you should read if you haven't already.

We have a particular "feminine genius,"[4] and it is resplendent with compassion, empathy, strength, and the ability to see another's point of view and bring their interests into play. Which makes even the simplest of life decisions, well, complicated.

Our prayer life is no exception. We download apps that will teach us how to pray and remind us when to pray and for whom we are praying. I have apps for the Bible, the Examen, the daily Mass readings, the Rosary, the Liturgy of the Hours, and the saints—to name a few. We can look up prayers in Latin and Spanish and listen to a daily reflection from the other side of the pond. We can find a Mass anywhere in the world and watch anything related to faith by pressing our finger on the screen. If you are like me, you spend as much time looking up prayer suggestions as you do actually praying.

We tend to play mind games with the simplest decisions. We move through the pros and cons of each choice as though they were pieces on a chessboard. Questions like *Should I apply for a new job? Get a new doctor? See a therapist? End a friendship? Change churches?* can escalate into rook-takes-knight, knight-takes-queen, and game-over before we've made our opening move.

Mary cultivated her faith life. By the time Gabriel appeared to her, she was already a faith-filled daughter of God.

Most questions are simple, but we overcomplicate them. Unlike Mary. She did five things that can help bring simplicity to our lives.

First, Mary cultivated her faith life. By the time Gabriel appeared to her, she was already a faith-filled daughter of God. We do not know exactly how she came to be this extraordinary young woman, but we can be certain that she had an open heart to encounter God in her Jewish rituals and that she nurtured a virtuous life animated by grace.

Second, Mary accepted God's vision of who she was and who she was meant to be.

My friend Sarah is an outgoing, speak-her-mind, quick-starting, set-the-world-on-fire, Catherine of Siena kind of girl. She often wishes she were more like the quiet and thoughtful Mother Theresa. But that's not who the Lord wants her to be, nor would it suit the good work she is doing in the world.

We are who we are, and we each have a unique mission in the world. Mary accepted hers, and the world was forever changed. Ponder this for a moment.

Third, Mary engaged her intellect. She wanted to know how these things would happen. She was inquisitive on a natural level yet discerning in the light of faith. Faith and reason are never at odds; they are unified by hope and trust.

Next, she implicitly trusted in God's plan. She did not consult her fears or worry about the future. She did not talk herself out of the mission God had for her. She trusted that God would use her unique gifts to change the world.

Lastly, she made a decision when she had the information she needed. Mary didn't talk to her parents, call out to her friends, or wonder what the neighbors would think. She didn't set up a poll to see who thought this was a good idea. She didn't ask for more time. She didn't run potential scenarios through her head.

Mary listened to the angel of the Lord whose name means "God is my strength," asked one little question, then uttered a simple *yes*. It not only changed her world but rocked the rest of ours too.

My set-the-world-on-fire friend, Sarah? After having her third child, she and her husband determined that they needed to simplify. For her, working full-time trying to change a corporate culture, being a supportive wife, and parenting wee ones made life too difficult. Like Mary, she asked, "How can this be?" Hard choices had to be made, with financial, social, and spiritual implications.

Sarah couldn't look at her vocations in a vacuum. She knew, as did St. John Paul II, that her work is part of a larger plan—God's plan. Making decisions with God at the center allowed worry to leave the conversation.

Sarah and her husband discerned that her work in the corporate world was God's mission for her: the fruit of her labor was incredibly abundant and necessary for the flourishing of many other families. Sarah's husband negotiated a part-time schedule, and the couple made some changes to simplify their life. An unforeseen bonus: their morning rush is gone, and they can pray together in the morning as a family. It's a new routine that has brought them closer as a couple.

Practical: Take Action

A complicated life leaves little time for the Lord. When I have demands and schedules to be met that leave me reading my Bible with drooping eyelids and an inattentive heart,

I know I need to simplify my schedule. Simplicity does not equal ease, however, and we know that. Mary's life had its share of challenges because of her *fiat*. But if you read her story, you see that she ponders all things in her heart and perseveres in her prayer. As we embrace her model, we too can be intentional in our choices.

How can simplicity operate in my life? Pray. Ponder. Think. Trust. Act. Like Mary, who asked Gabriel one question, ask the Lord—or yourself—one simple question: what do I need to change in order to simplify my life? Write down what comes to mind. Ponder the list. Think in "real life" possibilities. Trust in the process. Then take an action.

You may have more than one item in your needs-to-change basket, but for now select just one that you can commit to. For me, it's social media on my phone. It's not that catching up with the activities of my friends and family, laughing at some cute Catholic meme, or even learning something new isn't good; it can be. But such information can also clutter my heart, mind, and soul, complicate my life, and distract me from more important things.

Perhaps you need to reduce: declutter a closet, resign from a committee, decline an invitation, or resist the urge to shop online. Or perhaps you need to add something: use a day planner, set an alarm to begin a prayer time, or hire out a household chore. Choose one thing on your list, then set a date for accomplishing the task.

CHAPTER TWO

Martha

"Martha, Martha, you are anxious
and troubled about many things."
(Luke 10:41)

N ow as they went on their way, he entered a village; and a woman named Martha received him into her house. And she had a sister called Mary, who sat at the Lord's feet and listened to his teaching. But Martha was distracted with much serving; and she went to him and said, "Lord, do you not care that my sister has left me to serve alone? Tell her then to help me." But the Lord answered her, "Martha, Martha, you are anxious and troubled about many things; one thing is needful. Mary has chosen the good portion, which shall not be taken away from her." (Luke 10:38-42)

Scripture: Define the Passage

It was too warm of a morning to be walking back to town, regardless of the necessity of her errand. As the laundry list of things that needed to be finished before sundown grew to overflowing, she thought, *Why did I agree to this last-minute invitation to have Jesus over on the same day that I agreed to give these denarii to the Temple priests? What was I thinking?*

Bethany was known as the village where the sick and destitute came to find help and healing. Her mother once told her that *Beit Anya* (Bethany) means "house of the poor" or "house of welcome," so it was natural that the miserable came there to find rest from the weariness of the world. "Simon the leper" was among its inhabitants (see Matthew 26:6; Mark 14:3), though we can assume he was healed since he hosted people in his home.

We can imagine Martha taking on service of various sorts for the sick, perhaps even taking a few coins to the Temple priest so he could offer two pigeons to atone for a poor person's sin, in hopes for healing (see Leviticus 5:7-10). The sick couldn't go to the Temple, of course, as they needed to be kept away from the healthy.

Martha liked being known as the woman who could get things done. Her work gave her a sense of accomplishment. Her friend and mentor, Jesus, said that in serving others we serve God. "The kingdom of heaven is at hand," he said (Matthew 10:7). *Or it could be if everyone pitched in*, Martha thought.

Though serving others gave Martha immense pleasure, she was prone to taking on too many requests, which made for anxiety. She might agree to grind wheat for a neighbor in need, dye a batch of wool for someone's prayer shawl, and visit the poor. There were always plenty to visit. "You always have the poor with you," Jesus would say (Matthew 26:11), and it was true.

Martha's thoughts turned to the evening and the expected arrival of Jesus and his friends. She loved Jesus as her own brother, and she was delighted to welcome him and his friends into her home. The conversation would be deep, as Jesus always brought new meaning to God's word. It would be a lovely evening, she thought, if only there weren't so many things to do before Jesus and his companions arrived. How would she get it all done?

Martha's heart was heavy as she hurried to the market. The villagers' nods and smiles did not give her spirit the lift they normally did. She was "anxious and troubled about many things" (Luke 10:41).

Observe: Discover the Message

Reading this short story in Luke's Gospel, I focus on Martha. She is a woman of authority and means in the Jewish community.

Did you catch the fact that neither she nor Mary is married? Yet becoming a wife and mother is primary for Jewish women. Their brother Lazarus lives with them or perhaps nearby (see John 11:1-44), although he is not present in this story.

It would seem that Martha is a unique woman in her culture. She is a homeowner, single, with no children of her own, working in a poor town known for its almshouse. She fits no traditional category for Jewish women, and yet she is respected in the community.

Now as they went on their way, he entered a village;
and a woman named Martha received him into her
house. (Luke 10:38)

Martha opens her home to Jesus, welcoming him and
his disciples for an evening of fellowship. As the hostess, she would prepare the food, greet the guests, see to
their needs, and keep the lamps lit. She would have water
ready so that they could wash their dusty feet and quench
their thirst. There might be bread and olives and hummus
and wine on the table. Sufficient oil for the house's lamps
would be available.

Martha would appreciate her sister's help in keeping
Jesus and the disciples and perhaps other friends well
cared for.

She had a sister called Mary, who sat at the Lord's
feet and listened to his teaching. (Luke 10:39)

Mary, however, seems oblivious to the preparations. She
sits listening to what Jesus is saying. Doesn't she realize that
guests need to be fed? Surely the Lord will set things right.

Martha . . . went to him and said, "Lord, do you not
care that my sister has left me to serve alone? Tell
her then to help me." (Luke 10:40)

Notice that Martha doesn't come up behind her sister and whisper in her ear that she needs help. Nor does she make a "come here" motion to catch her sister's attention. No. Martha makes a scene. She points out to Jesus and everyone in the room that Mary is sitting when she should be helping with the tasks of a hostess: "Tell her then to help me" (Luke 10:40).

> But the Lord answered her, "Martha, Martha, you are anxious and troubled about many things; one thing is needful. Mary has chosen the good portion, which shall not be taken away from her." (Luke 10:41-42)

Words convey a deeper meaning than the letters that compose them. *Merimnao* ("anxious") indicates a deep preoccupation about something. It can indicate an ongoing worry that unsettles the soul.

The word *thorybazo* ("troubled") is also a word with depth. Some translators render it "distracted" or "disturbed." Martha isn't just worried about the refilling of water jugs or the distribution of work. *Merimnao* and *thorybazo* suggest that something deeper is working on her.

Jesus finishes with a gentle truth: "One thing is needful. Mary has chosen the good portion, which shall not be taken away from her" (Luke 10:42). Notice that Jesus doesn't tell Martha to stop working and join Mary. He just tells Martha that Mary has chosen wisely.

*A*pplication: Apply What You Learned

Distraction and worry are not what the Lord wants for us as we go about our work in the world. Jesus chides Martha not because she is unprepared for guests but because she is lacking something in her work, something that Mary knows is necessary and vital: *peace*. This is the most important thing we need as we carry out our day-to-day tasks.

The Hebrew word *shalom* is usually translated "peace." More than that, it denotes a peace rooted in one's relationship with God. It contains the underlying assumption that you are in a covenantal relationship with him. Therefore, no matter what happens in the world around you, there is no interior angst.

Shalom also denotes "completeness" and "wholeness." The quest for peace is a quest for human flourishing. In the social world, it follows justice. It can also include financial reward and the safety that security brings. In the soul, it is a word of blessing, of divine grace showered upon the person.

"Peace be with you," we say during Mass. Jesus could have said it to Martha in response to her rebuke of Mary. But instead, in typical Jesus style, he gets to the point: "You are anxious and troubled about many things" (Luke 10:41). What might Jesus know here?

Martha isn't feeling peaceful, and I get it. There is too much work for one person, and she feels overwhelmed.

She's doing the work of two women. It's not fair. She is frustrated and hurt, and she wants Jesus to acknowledge it: "Do you not care that my sister has left me to serve alone?" (Luke 10:40).

Martha isn't expected to stop working; she is to look at Jesus amid all that she does and remember that he is why she is working.

Jesus doesn't seem to care about Martha's well-being, but he definitely does. Jesus cares enough to get to the heart of the matter.

First he addresses the pride that comes with getting work done. Martha might be worried (*merimnao*) about her reputation. She wants validation. She wants Jesus to see her work and say, "Well done," or, "Great job," or, "This is why I keep coming back here."

This type of worry can make us snarky with our colleagues when mistakes are made. *We*, not Jesus, look good when something is perfect. We look for validation from our bosses, our families, the ladies in the lunchroom, and the lacrosse moms. Because we are doing a lot of work here, more than anyone else perhaps.

Second, Martha seems to have lost her center. She is distracted (*thorybazo*) by her tasks rather than the importance of the guests. Martha isn't expected to stop working; she is to look at Jesus amid all that she does and remember that *he* is why she is working. Her inner *shalom* is best when it radiates outward, filling the room with tranquility.

Jesus doesn't love us because of our *do*-ing. He loves us because of our *be*-ing. Martha forgot that, and we occasionally do too. We think that if we work hard enough and long enough, Jesus will see us. And if our work is good enough, he might even love us. This is a lie.

Jesus loves you, intimately and with reckless abandon, even when you are sick in bed with the flu and can hardly bring a tissue to your drippy nose or sip from a glass of water. He loves you even when you have a headache and can't crawl out from under the covers. He loves you even when you are incapacitated by a stroke or an accident or a random act of genetics that leaves you less than whole and unable to do what you once did. He loves you when your heart is broken over a death or divorce and you can hardly breathe, let alone put dinner on the table. He loves you even when you can't do anything.

Practical: Take Action

You belong to the Father. You are special to the Son. You stand out in the crowd to the Holy Spirit. To those three people who matter the most, you are a beloved daughter. It's not what you *do* that draws his gaze—it's who you are. In the end, Martha reclaims her inner tranquility. She enters into a deeper relationship with the Lord, which then allows her to meet the Lord in the midst of the chaos surrounding her brother's death. She gives what she has, which is abundant peace and hope in Jesus Christ, her Lord and Savior.

How can I bring more tranquility to my life? Jesus wants us, like Mary, to spend time with him. This week, carve out thirty minutes to pray with a psalm, perhaps Psalm 23 or 25, which speak of gentle protection, guidance, and kind assistance. Sit in a quiet place—maybe a corner of your home, in your car, on a park bench, or at Eucharistic Adoration. Begin with the Sign of the Cross, and take a moment to quiet your thoughts. Ask the Holy Spirit to guide your time.

Read the Scripture verses slowly and attentively. Make note of any word, phrase, or image that catches your attention. You may want to read the passage out loud to help you focus. Reflect on what draws your mind and heart. Let the Lord speak directly to you. What is he saying to you through this text?

Entrust your needs and concerns to the Lord, and make note of any action he is asking you to take. Finally, thank him for the blessings he has shown you, and rest for a few minutes in his presence.

CHAPTER THREE

The Woman Caught in Adultery

The scribes and the Pharisees brought a woman who had been caught in adultery, . . . placing her in the midst. (John 8:3)

Early in the morning he came again to the temple; all the people came to him, and he sat down and taught them. The scribes and the Pharisees brought a woman who had been caught in adultery, and placing her in the midst they said to him, "Teacher, this woman has been caught in the act of adultery. Now in the law Moses commanded us to stone such. What do you say about her?" This they said to test him, that they might have some charge to bring against him. Jesus bent down and wrote with his finger on the ground. And as they continued to ask him, he stood up and said to them, "Let him who is without sin among you be the first to throw a stone at her." And once more he bent down and wrote with his finger on the ground. But when they heard it, they went away, one by one, beginning with the eldest, and Jesus was left alone with the woman standing before him. Jesus looked up and said to her, "Woman, where are they? Has no one condemned you?" She said, "No one, Lord." And Jesus said, "Neither do I condemn you; go, and do not sin again." (John 8:2-11)

Scripture: Define the Passage

How did this happen? she thinks. *Where did all these men come from?* Head down, afraid to meet anyone's eyes, she glances at feet and sandals, knowing which belong to whom. The baker is here, and so is the blacksmith. She thinks they are smiling. Her uncle is here too. She sees the hem of her childhood friend's cloak, the one whose arms held her as she cried during the weeks after her parents died. Tears begin to run down her cheeks.

She thinks the onlookers will assume that repentance and fear cause the tears, but it is anger, embarrassment, resentment, and shame that she feels: anger that her uncle arranged a marriage without her consent; embarrassment for the way the other women stop talking when she comes to the well; resentment for the way her life has unfolded; shame at her own sin. These emotions make her feel small, very small. Tears run down her unveiled face.

What will they say about her? She knows they are using her as bait to lure this unsuspecting prophet into deciding a matter of law. The scribes even now talk about trapping the poor man.

Stumbling across the Temple courtyard, she feels the eyes of the men regarding her with contempt. She is guilty of being with a man who is not her husband. She wonders if that man is here too. The Law of Moses requires the stoning of both the man and the woman caught lying with each other. But she doesn't hear his voice or see him among the men.

It is a trap, she thinks, for the prophet and for her. The baker and the blacksmith are smiling. *They don't like either one of us.*

Perhaps God will allow for a sudden thunderstorm, and she will be struck by lightning. *Please, God, let this be*, she prays. *They are going to stone me to death anyway. Does life even matter anymore? No*, she thinks. *It doesn't.*

Observe: Discover the Message

The Gospel according to John has several dualistic markers: light is good, darkness is bad; the flesh is bad, but the spirit is good; there is truth, and there are lies; believers in Jesus will have eternal life, and nonbelievers will not. The priests and scribes of the Temple and the lowly people of God are at odds. God and Satan battle over souls.

In one of the most stunning pieces of poetry ever written, John opens his Gospel by uniting the Father and the Son in a perfect union of mind and thought: "In the beginning was the Word, and the Word was with God, and the Word was God" (John 1:1). Jesus *is* God. And the Word of God cares deeply about the lives of individual people.

Jesus' presence in the world is a unique blend of power and compassion. He is a powerful man made for a gentle encounter. The one who says, "I am the way, and the truth, and the life," also says, "Let not your hearts be troubled" (John 14:6, 1).

John uses some form of the word "abide" (*meno*) nearly seventy times. To *meno* is to dwell, lodge, remain, sojourn, endure, exist, or await. This abiding is constant, steadfast, and persevering. It is an intimate and settled union. It is a permanent state of relationship with a powerful yet tender source.

John also uses everyday words and common experiences to denote a change of heart. For a world that is in darkness half the time, Jesus is the light of the world (8:12). For a people who live off the land and sea, Jesus is the bread of life and the source of living water (6:35; 7:37-38). For the agrarian society, Jesus is the Good Shepherd whose sheep hear his voice. He is the gate, the door, and the way (10:1-9). He is the vine, and we are the branches (15:5). Ours is an intimate relationship with the all-encompassing Love Incarnate.

> Early in the morning he came again to the temple. (John 8:2)

The story of the woman caught in adultery, a very intimate act, happens early in the morning, as the sun begins to rise. We move from darkness into light. Something remarkable is about to happen.

> All the people came to him, and he sat down and taught them. (John 8:2)

The temple guards have explained to the Pharisees just the day before why they were unsuccessful in their attempt to arrest Jesus (see John 7:45-46). The Temple elite had their own "force," often translated as officers, police, or guards. When these found Jesus, he was surrounded by people who loved his words and his presence. The guards too listened for a bit, which made them reluctant to arrest him.

These officers told the chief priests and Pharisees, "No man ever spoke like this man!" (John 7:46). The Pharisees responded in disgust, "Are you led astray, you also?" (John 7:47). The well-known Nicodemus spoke up in defense of the guards but was roundly dismissed. The stage is set for conflict.

Let us try to picture this scene of Jesus and the woman caught in adultery. One thing to note is that the sun will rise in the east, its rays expanding over a Temple courtyard the size of six football fields. Designated areas are reserved for sacrifice, study of *Torah* and other rabbinic texts, and relaxation. Men and women have their personal sections. At one end of the Temple is the Holy of Holies, the inner sanctum that holds the ark of the covenant. Only the high priest can enter this veiled area and only once a year, on the Day of Atonement.

It is here, in the center of intellectual, social, and spiritual realms, where Jesus is quietly teaching in the morning hours. Plenty of men are in the courtyard listening to him. Faithful men come here to pray and to discuss Moses and the Law and how the Law should be administered in individual cases. And here is a case at the ready.

> The scribes and the Pharisees brought a woman who had been caught in adultery. (John 8:3)

This is an ordinary Jewish woman, *gyne* in Greek, not a prostitute (*porne*). She was caught "in the act" of committing adultery. How exactly is one caught in the very act—unless someone is waiting and watching for the tryst to occur? This would seem to indicate a trap.

The scribes and Pharisees have been looking for a way to discredit and arrest Jesus, then scatter his followers. Sending their armed guards didn't work, so they devise another way.

> And placing her in the midst they said to him, "Teacher, this woman has been caught in the act of adultery." (John 8:3-4)

What might this woman be wearing, and how might she look, having been taken from this intimate encounter to the Temple courtyard? How might she have arrived?

The word "brought" is a translation of *ago*, which is often used in shepherding to mean "bring," "lead away," or "drive off." It presupposes a context of force: to hurry along, to drag, or to incite and entice. Our woman is "brought" into the Temple courtyard, made to stand before all while the Pharisees tell her story.

> "Now in the law Moses commanded us to stone such. What do you say about her?" (John 8:5)

The Pharisees want to make a scene. Jesus knows the laws of Judaism, as he has been schooled in them by his parents and elders. Surely he knows that Moses came down from Mount Sinai after speaking with God and that one of the Ten Commandments is "Do not commit adultery."

Jesus also knows the prescriptive punishments for disobedience, the penal codes of Deuteronomy, which were also given by God to Moses on Mount Sinai. The penal codes say that if a man is found lying with a woman who is not his wife, they both should be taken to the city gates and stoned to death (Deuteronomy 22:22). Yet the Pharisees only bring the woman to Jesus.

> Jesus bent down and wrote with his finger on the ground. (John 8:6)

At first Jesus ignores the Pharisees' question of law. Instead he bends down and writes on the ground with his finger. He ignores the chatter and the gossip and the innuendoes. There are lots of men in that courtyard, remember. There are those who came to hear Jesus speak and those who came to speak their mind.

> And as they continued to ask him, he stood up and said to them, "Let him who is without sin among you be the first to throw a stone at her." And once more he bent down and wrote with his finger on the ground. (John 8:7-8)

Jesus addresses the situation. In the Jewish court of law, two or three witnesses are needed to establish fact from fiction. Then, "the hand of the witnesses shall be first against him to put him to death" (Deuteronomy 17:7). In addition, to prevent lying and preserve justice, false accusers are subject to the same penalty as the one accused would have been given (see Deuteronomy 19:16-19).

Jesus stands and tells the Pharisees to go ahead and throw their stones if they are sinless in this matter and others. He never answers their direct question on the validity of the law; he activates their sense of justice and mercy by example. Nor does he shame and berate the scribes and the Pharisees.

He asks them only to live out the Golden Rule, which is to treat others as they would be treated (Matthew 7:12). He asks them to live out their Great *Sh'ma Yisrael* (Deuteronomy 6:4-9): to love the Lord their God with all their hearts, with all their souls, and with all their might; and then to love their neighbors as themselves (Leviticus 19:18). If they are going to quote the Law to him, they should pay attention to its entirety.

Jesus bends down and returns to writing on the ground. Some biblical scholars intuit that Jesus was writing down the sins of the men who stood before him. Some older texts extend John 8:8 to read: "And once again, he bent down and wrote on the ground the sins of each of them."[5] Perhaps he simply begins to write out sins, not attaching names to them. Jeremiah 17:13 might have been in Jesus' mind:

> All who forsake thee shall be put to shame;
> those who turn away from thee shall be written in the earth,
> for they have forsaken the LORD, the fountain of living water.

Jesus gives the woman's accusers a credible way out of the confrontation. He creates a win-win proposition. He asks them to see the woman standing in front of them, look at her worth and dignity, and compare those to their own. He reminds them that law must be of service to dignity and seen by the light of love. That is true justice.

> When they heard it, they went away, one by one, beginning with the eldest, and Jesus was left alone with the woman standing before him. (John 8:9)

The scribes and Pharisees walk away, as do the people who had come to hear him speak. Everyone is a sinner.

> Jesus looked up and said to her, "Woman, where are they? Has no one condemned you?" She said, "No one, Lord." And Jesus said, "Neither do I condemn you; go, and do not sin again." (John 8:10-11)

Jesus doesn't let this woman off the hook. "Has no one condemned you?" he asks. At which she must look around the empty courtyard, with love and gratitude, and say, "No one." Jesus then says that he does not condemn her either, but she must not sin again.

In the very next line of the Gospel, Jesus says, "I am the light of the world" (John 8:12). This describes a remarkable happening in the Temple courtyard: the light has banished the darkness.

Application: Apply What You Learned

When a woman reaches a certain age and looks back on her life, she might see at least one moment when she could have "died from embarrassment." Perhaps it was lipstick on a tooth during a coveted interview, being caught in an intentional untruth, or passing along a bit of gossip that ruined a relationship. Maybe it was a surprising, very public, and unwanted breakup or a trip to the city jail when she was certain she had been under the limit. Maybe a teen daughter became pregnant. Or maybe her world was rocked when a text revealed a sexual infidelity.

Chances are, we've either been this woman caught in sin, acted as a scribe or Pharisee bringing it to light, or stood in the crowd watching the scene unfold. Either we've been ashamed and humiliated, or we've watched it happen.

We also know women whose dignity meters have never been calibrated to acceptable levels. Long-term emotional and physical abuse tend to make the distortions reality. Perhaps we've been told that we are too slender or too weighted when we are not. The truth about us is not always apparent to the world around us. We've been told we are worthless when we are valued by the Father. We're reminded that our failures are unforgiveable when all was forgiven on the cross.

Jesus certainly changes the way the woman in John 8 might feel about herself. There are a few things here that we can learn about dignity.

Let's imagine what Jesus might be saying to the men gathered around him in the early morning hours. He knows what is about to transpire. Morning prayer might include something from the psalms:

> O LORD, thou hast searched me and known me! . . .
> For thou didst form my inward parts,
>   thou didst knit me together in my mother's womb.
> I praise thee, for thou art fearful and wonderful.
>   Wonderful are thy works! (Psalm 139:1, 13, 14).

With the beginning of a new day, Jesus might choose the poetry of creation: "So God created man in his own image, in the image of God he created him; male and female he created them" (Genesis 1:27). Or a snippet from the prophet Micah:

> He has showed you . . . what is good;
>   and what does the LORD require of you
> but to do justice, and to love kindness,
>   and to walk humbly with your God? (Micah 6:8)

These are words of hope and strength for a soul struggling to know dignity. They are words of guidance for men too ready to pass judgment, for Pharisees who want to create a scene, to publicly condemn and humiliate.

Perhaps we've passed by someone on a busy corner with a tin cup or a cardboard sign that reads, "Will work for food." I distinctly remember one such woman. In a hurry and late to pick up my daughter from school, I took the freeway into the city. Normally I would take the more scenic suburban route, but I needed to fast-track the drive. It was Minnesota spring day, so my windows were down. As I took the exit ramp and readied to make the quick right, I heard the booming voice: "Whatcha doin' there, girl? Why dontcha get it right?"

The woman was standing in the middle of the concrete median on a busy street. She was thin, unkempt, tattooed.

She started out standing tall as could be, eyes straight forward, while this guy yelled at her through a megaphone. I watched her resolve fade and her dignity crumble. She reminded me of our woman standing in the middle of the Temple courtyard surrounded by her accusers.

We all experience times of isolation and loss of dignity, because we all tumble every now and again. We make a mistake, break a vow, give in to a vice, cave to a bad habit, even do something we never thought we would do. We feel miserable afterward. We understand the consequences. We think, *I can't believe I did that. How did this happen? Who knows about this? Who saw that?* One unanswered question leads to another, one dismal thought to another, and we find ourselves alone and in the dark.

It doesn't matter where you come from or what you did; it's who you are that Jesus is interested in.

Satan loves to step in when we sin and add to our feelings of worthlessness and isolation. *Surely*, he accuses, *you will sin again. And God will not forgive you. Surely*, he affirms, *you have no dignity or worth.*

Do not listen to this voice. Satan lies.

When condemning voices whisper in the darkness, remember the woman caught in adultery. Jesus came to her defense. He condemned not her but her sin. He knows the difference between actions and persons.

You are the light of his world. It doesn't matter where you come from or what you did; it's who you are that Jesus is interested in. You are beautiful in the eyes of God. Jesus stands next to you, protecting you, saving you, loving you. No matter what.

I don't know what happened to the woman caught in adultery, and I don't know what happened to the woman in the median. I was one of those folks in the crowd who came to hear Jesus speak and then left the scene to ponder my part in the drama. The car behind me blared its horn, and I sped off, thinking I would swing back after picking up my daughter. Which I didn't do. And so this memory haunts me.

Practical: Take Action

Dignity is not a singular notion. By this I mean it is a compilation of words and ideas given to us throughout our lives, which we, in turn, internalize. It's a word that Jesus didn't know—there is no Hebrew or Aramaic equivalent—but it's a notion that women have fought for throughout time. We see it in the real lives of women in the Gospels and in our lives today. It's a word of courage, filled with other words like grace, fulfillment, imperfection, self-respect, poise, and virtue. It is bestowed upon us before we were knit in our mother's wombs by the One whose love strengthens and sustains us. Dignity is within us and in those we encounter in our lives.

How might a robust sense of dignity operate in my life? Living with an awareness of your dignity can be much more difficult if you are weighed down by some hurt, pain, or resentment. Light a candle, then take a moment to think about past life choices that are weighing you down. Say a prayer asking the Lord for forgiveness, then blow out the candle. Watch that prayer float to the Lord in the smoke. Ask him to lift your burden and grant you the courage to forgive yourself.

Consider going to Reconciliation. Or you may want to make a personal appointment with a priest or a trusted spiritual mentor, to allow more time to talk about what is weighing you down and to receive God's gift of healing.

Whatever you are carrying, take a minute now to invite God to give you the grace to step out and move forward, embracing your dignity and worth as his beloved child.

CHAPTER FOUR

Mary Magdalene

Now on the first day of the week
Mary Magdalene came to the tomb
early, while it was still dark.
(John 20:1)

Nicodemus . . . , who had at first come to him by night, came bringing a mixture of myrrh and aloes, about a hundred pounds' weight. They took the body of Jesus, and bound it in linen cloths with the spices, as is the burial custom of the Jews. Now in the place where he was crucified there was a garden, and in the garden a new tomb where no one had ever been laid. So because of the Jewish day of Preparation, as the tomb was close at hand, they laid Jesus there.

Now on the first day of the week Mary Magdalene came to the tomb early, while it was still dark, and saw that the stone had been taken away from the tomb. So she ran, and went to Simon Peter and the other disciple, the one whom Jesus loved, and said to them, "They have taken the Lord out of the tomb, and we do not know where they have laid him." Peter then came out with the other disciple, and they went toward the tomb. They both ran, but the other disciple outran Peter and reached the tomb first; and stooping to look in, he saw the linen cloths lying there, but he did not go in. Then Simon Peter came, following him, and went into the tomb; he saw the linen cloths lying, and the napkin, which had been on his head, not lying with the linen cloths but rolled up in a place by itself. Then the other disciple, who reached the tomb first, also went in, and he saw and believed; for as yet they did not know the scripture, that he must rise from the dead. Then the disciples went back to their homes.

But Mary stood weeping outside the tomb, and as she wept she stooped to look into the tomb; and she saw two angels in white, sitting where the body of Jesus had lain, one at the head and one at the feet. They said to her, "Woman, why are you weeping?" She said to them, "Because they have taken away my Lord, and I do not know where they have laid him." Saying this, she turned round and saw Jesus standing, but she did not know that it was Jesus. Jesus said to her, "Woman, why are you weeping? Whom do you seek?" Supposing him to be the gardener, she said to him, "Sir, if you have carried him away, tell me where you have laid him, and I will take him away." Jesus said to her, "Mary." She turned and said to him in Hebrew, "Rab-bo'ni!" (which means Teacher). Jesus said to her, "Do not hold me, for I have not yet ascended to the Father; but go to my brethren and say to them, I am ascending to my Father and your Father, to my God and your God." Mary Magdalene went and said to the disciples, "I have seen the Lord"; and she told them that he had said these things to her. (John 19:39–20:18)

Scripture: Define the Passage

Mary dropped to the floor in sheer exhaustion, the smell of myrrh and aloe still clinging to her.

Exhaustion. Mary thought she knew this word from her time with Jesus, traveling from place to place, providing food, washing clothes, listening to his teaching. Learning, laughing, loving. It was an exciting time. It was hard work, to be sure, and many nights her head hit the straw mat gratefully.

Exhaustion. It was the way she felt when those demons had lived within her. Then Jesus came to Magdala. He was her Savior, the Teacher, the Healer, the Son of God Most High. He set her free. He restored her dignity and gave her friendship and authentic love.

Mary became a new woman. Now she had friends to laugh with, to walk with, and to share bread and wine with. The past three years of following Jesus were a blur of towns and temples, preaching and healing, insights and instruction.

It was a time of contentment that she had hoped would never end. But it did, violently. Mary stood with his mother at the foot of the cross while few others would. Like the other women who chastely loved him, she felt the nails enter, she felt the groans deep within her heart, she heard the rending of the tunic, she tasted the bitter vinegar, and yes, she witnessed the final departure of the soul. It all left her feeling dark and empty.

She assisted Joseph and Nicodemus in binding Jesus' body with the burial cloths and applying the spices. After tucking the last strip of cloth under the others, they laid his body in the cold tomb, then moved the stone in place. "It is finished" had been Jesus' last words, and so it was (John 19:30).

And now Mary lay crumpled in a ball in the dark of night, unable to move, hardly able to draw breath, mentally and physically exhausted and alone. Thus would she pass her sabbath rest.

Observe: Discover the Message

The Gospel according to John, written at the turn of the century, has several dualistic markers, as noted in the previous chapter. The time of its composition was a dangerous era for the early followers of Jesus. Persecutions abounded. Saul had Stephen stoned, Nero had Paul beheaded, and the rest of the disciples (except John) met untimely demises. None of the early Christian communities were spared; the grief and loss touched everyone. They followed the way of the Master, publicly condemned and crucified.

> Nicodemus . . . , who had at first come to him by night,
> came bringing a mixture of myrrh and aloes, about
> a hundred pounds' weight. (John 19:39)

Most of the disciples abandoned Jesus. "His mother, and his mother's sister, Mary the wife of Clopas, and Mary Magdalene" were with Jesus to the end, along with "the disciple whom he loved" (John 19:25, 26). The Pharisees Joseph of Arimathea and Nicodemus removed Jesus from the cross and laid him in a tomb. This is the same Nicodemus, John writes, who first came to Jesus by night (19:39).

The Jewish custom was to bury the dead immediately, covering the body with myrrh, spices, and aromatic ointments—such as aloe, balsam, cumin, cassia, cinnamon, and spikenard. Nicodemus arrives with a mixture of myrrh and aloes, weighing about a hundred pounds. The number of burial scents used is in direct proportion to social standing. A common burial, like that of Lazarus (see John 11), might use a pound at most. Jesus is truly the Beloved.

> They took the body of Jesus, and bound it in linen
> cloths with the spices, as is the burial custom of the
> Jews. Now in the place where he was crucified there
> was a garden, and in the garden a new tomb where
> no one had ever been laid. So . . . they laid Jesus there.
> (John 19:40-42)

Mary and friends lay Jesus' body in the tomb carved in the mountainside. A large stone is rolled in front to keep Jesus in and everyone else out.

Did you catch that? Jesus' followers prepared and buried Jesus just as they would anyone else who died. They did not expect him to rise from the dead. If they anticipated the resurrection, they would have dressed him in a clean tunic and left a pair of sandals at the tomb, don't you think?

> On the first day of the week . . . early, while it was still dark. (John 20:1)

Mary comes to the tomb in the early morning darkness, alone. This is unusual. Jewish women were not permitted to travel alone, particularly before the sun rose. Our modern imagination presupposes a lit trail or an easily identifiable path—neither of which was probably the case.

Mary may be walking on somewhat familiar ground; perhaps she carries a candle. We can imagine her feeling her way through the darkness while sifting through her emotions. Our experience with John's Gospel leads us to the thought that Mary is also trying to find her way through spiritual darkness.

> Mary Magdalene came . . . and saw that the stone had been taken away from the tomb. So she ran, and

> went to Simon Peter and the other disciple, the one
> whom Jesus loved. (John 20:1-2)

Mary's first response on seeing the tomb with the stone off to the side is to run to Simon Peter and the beloved disciple. Notice that she doesn't look in the tomb. She makes the assumption that someone has taken the body, then goes to seek corroboration. Peter and the beloved disciple run to the tomb. Peter enters and finds the linen cloths but no Jesus. Then John enters, and he "saw and believed" (20:8).

Time is passing here in the wee morning hours as these events unfold. The sun is beginning to appear over the horizon, and the world is becoming brighter.

> Then the disciples went back to their homes.
> But Mary stood weeping outside the tomb. (John
> 20:10-11)

Something is amiss. Who would take a decomposing body and leave the wrappings behind?

Mary has covered miles in her two visits to the tomb. She is both mentally and physically exhausted. She remains rooted to the spot outside the tomb, weeping with confusion and wrapped in her grief.

> As she wept she stooped to look into the tomb; and
> she saw two angels in white, sitting where the body
> of Jesus had lain, one at the head and one at the
> feet. (John 20:11-12)

Mary needs verification. She needs to see things with her own eyes—to touch the linen cloths, smell the scents she lovingly covered his body with, and linger in the tomb. She wants to see what Peter and John have seen, perhaps to try and make sense of it all. She stoops to look inside.

And she is surprised by what she sees: two angels, or messengers, clothed in white, sitting at each end of the burial slab. The word "white" is *leukos*, which lends itself to pure light or brightness. "Two messengers, emanating the light of God" might be a more apt description.

> They said to her, "Woman, why are you weeping?" (John 20:13)

The angels speak as if they do not know why Mary mourns and where her Beloved now stands. Mary replies that someone has taken Jesus' body to a new tomb, and "I do not know where they have laid him" (John 20:13). She expects to find the body elsewhere in this burial garden, as she cannot imagine that anyone could have carried a corpse very far.

> Saying this, she turned round and saw Jesus standing, but she did not know that it was Jesus. (John 20:14)

Mary still stands outside the hewn tomb, bending over, speaking to the angels inside. Perhaps the angels are looking beyond her to where Jesus is standing. Mary follows their gaze, turns her head, and sees Jesus. He asks her the same question the angels asked: "Woman, why are you weeping?" and adds, "Whom do you seek?" (John 20:15).

Between her grief and exhaustion and his transformation, Mary doesn't recognize Jesus. Supposing he is the gardener, she glances away, perhaps at the empty slab, and asks that if he is the one who carried her Beloved away, could he direct her to the place, so she can retrieve the body?

> Jesus said to her, "Mary." She turned and said to him in Hebrew, "Rabboni!" (John 20:16)

"Mary," Jesus whispers, gentle and kind, with a love that awakens her. "Mary." It is her name, as she has heard him say it a hundred times. She turns to where that familiar voice comes from.

Mary is transformed from a woman of grief to a woman of joy.

The word "turns" is *strepho*. It means more than a turn of the physical body. It is most often used to indicate a change in substance. Water *strepho* into steam. Wine *strepho* into blood. Bread *strepho* into flesh. It is to change one's course of action based on a new principle, to be converted in heart, mind, and soul.

Mary does not just turn her physical body to see Jesus; she is internally changed, converted, illuminated by truth.

She is transformed from a woman of grief to a woman of joy.

"Rabboni!" Mary exclaims, in full recognition of her Beloved. She seems ready to fall into a gentle and intimate embrace. Jesus, however, asks of her a difficult task: she must let go of him again, as she did from the foot of the cross.

> "Do not hold me, for I have not yet ascended to the Father; but go to my brethren and say to them, I am ascending to my Father and your Father, to my God and your God." (John 20:17)

Jesus sends Mary on mission to the other disciples, to tell them what is to happen: that he is to ascend to "my Father and your Father, to my God and your God." The sun and the Son have now risen.

Exhausted no more, Mary runs off in the light of day to tell the good news to the disciples.

Application: Apply What You Learned

Exhaustion often creeps into our lives under cover of grief or busyness, which masquerades as overcommitment but really can be something more insidious. Exhaustion is an internal response to external events, some of which we have control over but many of which we do not.

We are caregivers and nurses to those we love. We are teachers and parents and mentors to those who need our wisdom. We are managers and business owners who have employees looking to us for direction and decisions. We are mothers and grandmothers and aunts who are responsible for nurturing life. We are wives caring for ill husbands and daughters looking out for our mothers. We are grieving mothers and widows.

In all our roles, no matter what the title, it sometimes happens that we awake in the predawn hours, like Mary Magdalene, unable to sleep.

Sometimes we are one unsuspected life challenge away from a breakdown. Perhaps it will be a red light on the dashboard, a client who drops our firm, a mammogram callback, a divorce decree, or the death of a loved one.

Sometimes it starts like a simple mathematical word problem: "Your mom is leaving the rehab unit at 7:30 a.m. and needs to travel thirty miles westward to her home. Your boss expects you to lead a meeting at 8:00 a.m., for which you need to make a twenty-mile eastward commute. The nurse should call with your test results before noon, and your daughter isn't feeling well. At what time do they all collide?"

I've never been good at word problems, but I do know that these are the problems that become I-can't-do-this-anymore thoughts.

Mary of Magdala's world collapsed over the course of a few days, and there was nothing she could do about it. She had been walking through the countryside with Jesus and his disciples, and then she wasn't. There was no time to process or plan, and that is when exhaustion set in.

When exhaustion hits, we, like Mary, can feel alone and abandoned. We can't sleep. We can't talk to friends.

Mary went to the tomb alone and in the dark. John gives us no real cause for her heading there. She was drawn, perhaps, by the desire to find comfort in her Lord. So can we be drawn when we are exhausted by the twists and turns of life, even a life well lived and well ordered. Because healing comes in the presence of the Lord.

Mary brings her assumptions about herself and her world to the tomb. The angels want her to ponder the source of her tears. She gives a correct yet superficial answer: "They have taken away my Lord, and I do not know where they have laid him" (20:13). Jesus asks her the same question, and she gives a similar answer. She does not say, "My peace, my joy, my love is gone. I am devasted. I am exhausted with grief."

We sometimes go to the Lord with reasons for our exhaustion. *I have a more-than-full-time-job, I have a wedding to plan, the baby has an ear infection, the engine blew in the car, the kids' sports schedules have more times than hours in the day, my mom will enter hospice soon.* Something has stolen our peace and joy. Some variable, some event, or some life challenge has entered our lives, and we are now officially exhausted and alone in the dark.

Did you notice that Mary never enters the tomb? She stoops down and peers in but doesn't walk all the way in to take a real look around.

Like Mary, sometimes we are rooted in our own places, in our own exhaustion, unable to go into our own personal tomb of darkness. Perhaps it is the death of a loved one, the drama of an illness, or an addiction we cannot battle alone. Past hurts, regrets, or actions can lie buried deep inside, and we wonder what might happen if they are brought to the light. We stoop to look in the tomb where we've hidden our darkest hours, but do we cross that threshold?

No, thank you. We're afraid of what we might find if we go further. We can't take one more surprise.

But the messengers of God ask us to do just that: to peer inside, to seek the truth. "Why are you weeping?" they ask. Jesus asks the same question of Mary and of us: "Woman, why are you weeping?"

In our grief and exhaustion, we often lack clarity. We only see our mess and our pain and our suffering. In his infinite love and mercy, Jesus feeds us the answer in question form: "Whom do you seek?" Yes. The answer isn't a myriad of reasons why we weep—the Lord knows those. He wants us to look toward him.

"Mary." The sound of her name draws Mary away from things that do not matter and toward him who matters above all. We too can turn and reorient ourselves to the One who really matters. In the turning, we base our actions and emotions not on the external things that happen but on our internal well-being, on the One who loves us beyond all comprehension.

Once Mary turns to face her Beloved, Jesus gives her yet another task: go and tell the others. Her grief and exhaustion will ease, and she has a new mission. This task will have struggles, along with unexpected and unwelcome surprises. Life will still be complicated and full of twists and turns, some of them unfortunate and beyond her control. She will be exhausted by grief, but it will pass.

As a matter of fact, Mary will be renowned throughout history, and her story will be remembered long after she is gone from this earth. She will be called "the apostle of the apostles," and women and men alike will turn to her in prayer, asking her to carry their intentions to Jesus.

They will look to her example for strength, grace, perseverance, and wisdom. They will follow her example and be witnesses to the world. Her name will be spoken by the successors of Peter, and her reputation will be protected by the greatest of all men.

Practical: Take Action

Mary of Magdala is a woman who lost the physical presence of her traveling companion, her mentor, her teacher, her Savior, and most importantly, the One she loved above all else. Mary probably grieved for the physical presence of Jesus throughout her life and felt exhausted even *after* encountering the Lord outside the empty tomb. I imagine some mornings she rose while it was still dark, unable to sleep. But I imagine her exhaustion and grief felt different, as it was infused with the hope of letting go and letting God lead.

What is it you need to let go of? You likely have had to let go of something without being wholeheartedly ready or willing to do the letting go. Perhaps a loved one has died. Perhaps an event or relationship didn't turn out the way you expected. Perhaps you mourn a wayward child or family member.

Close your eyes, and invite the Lord into your home. Sit with him as you would with your best friend. Begin a conversation over coffee and scones, talking in your head, or aloud, or writing the exchange in your journal. Share with him your burdens and your grief. Allow yourself to be honest with him about the disappointment that you feel. Jesus knows the exhaustion of grief intimately. "Jesus wept" when he was at the tomb of Lazarus, his dear friend (John 11:35). When you have said all that needs to be healed, place your hands in front of you, palms up, offering all your cares. Let him reach across the table, gently fold your hands together, and place his around yours, while whispering your name. Imagine the relief. Your burdens are safe with God.

CHAPTER FIVE

The Hemorrhaging Woman

She had heard the reports about
Jesus, and came up behind him
in the crowd and touched his
garment. (Mark 5:27)

And a great crowd followed him and thronged about him. And there was a woman who had had a flow of blood for twelve years, and who had suffered much under many physicians, and had spent all that she had, and was no better but rather grew worse. She had heard the reports about Jesus, and came up behind him in the crowd and touched his garment. For she said, "If I touch even his garments, I shall be made well." And immediately the hemorrhage ceased; and she felt in her body that she was healed of her disease. And Jesus, perceiving in himself that power had gone forth from him, immediately turned about in the crowd, and said, "Who touched my garments?" And his disciples said to him, "You see the crowd pressing around you, and yet you say, 'Who touched me?'" And he looked around to see who had done it. But the woman, knowing what had been done to her, came in fear and trembling and fell down before him, and told him the whole truth. And he said to her, "Daughter, your faith has made you well; go in peace, and be healed of your disease." (Mark 5:24-34)

Scripture: Define the Passage

It wasn't the illness itself that was the problem; it was the loneliness. The stains on her garments were a visible reminder to the world that she was sick and untouchable. *Don't talk to her. You might catch what she has. She's unclean, dirty, sin-filled.*

She could not bear the isolation, the lack of community and conversation. She longed for the presence of other women in her life—for laughter and tears and stories shared. She was desperate for companionship and friendship.

Only the doctors whose varied ideas about how to stop the constant flow of blood came to her, with their treatments and tools. Oh, the things her body endured. She saw the scars as battle wounds. In some ways, she was a stronger and braver woman because of them.

One day, as she walked toward the water with her basket of stained linens, one of the elders was sitting in the shade of a fig tree. He made a sound as she walked by, and for some reason she glanced his way, wondering if she would receive pity or persecution. She saw kindness in his eyes. He motioned for her to come closer. She turned to look behind her, as surely he could not mean her. But the road was empty. He was beckoning her to come closer.

She came as close as she dared, ready to run away quickly if necessary. This man knew about her, of course. Everyone knew to avoid her. But he looked at her with unusually kind eyes. He told her about a man named Jesus who healed the deaf, the blind, and the lame. Jesus was in the area, he said, and she should go and talk to him. She looked at the man with disbelief and some suspicion. Was this a trap?

Men were not allowed to talk to any non-family women, let alone an unclean woman like her. Yes, he told her, this man talks to women in the open. He has many who support and provide for him—one from the town of Magdala, out of whom he had cast seven demons.

"Jesus can heal you too," he said, looking her directly in the eye. He was so confident in his manner and his tone that she believed him. Then came the sound of footsteps, and the elder cast his eyes to the ground. "Go," he said, and she did.

She would find this Jesus. Even if he were in a crowd, she would approach him. She would tolerate the whisperings, the stares, the people backing away. She would find this Jesus. If the elder was right and this man had power, then maybe, just maybe, she could get close enough to touch him, and she would be made well. Then she could have a friend and be a friend.

Observe: Discover the Message

There was a woman who had had a flow of blood for twelve years. (Mark 5:25)

The woman with a hemorrhage appears in all three synoptic Gospels, and in all cases the healing occurs as Jesus walks to the house of Jairus to raise his young daughter from the dead. If you read further in Mark's Gospel, you'll notice that the daughter is twelve years old (see Mark 5:42). And this woman has been ill for twelve years.

What do you think of when you hear the words "twelve" and "Jesus"? The age of Jesus when his parents found him in the Temple (see Luke 2:41-46)? The number of baskets of bread left over after he fed the five thousand (Matthew 14:20)? The number of chosen apostles (Luke 6:13-16)?

> *In the Jewish mind, twelve is a number of completion—totality or wholeness, according to the will of God.*

In the Jewish mind, twelve is a number of completion—totality or wholeness, according to the will of God. When we read the word "twelve" in a story, we know something remarkable is about to happen.

Listeners in the early Church would also know that this vignette is less about the physical healing of the bleeding woman and more about her reinstatement into community life. Blood was, and is, a sign of life. Losing blood meant that you were "losing life."

The presence of blood isolated a person from community life. A bleeding person, whether man or woman, was confined to the home. Leviticus tells us that every place on which a bleeding woman sat or lay was unclean. If a man sat where she had sat, he was unclean until evening. If a man shared a bed with her, he was unclean for seven days (see Leviticus 15:20-24). An unclean person could not interact with anyone else, in order to protect the purity of the community (15:31).

The hemorrhaging woman has not been in the presence of her family or friends for twelve years—twelve years of isolation and loneliness. No hugs or handshakes or human embrace.

> [She] had suffered much under many physicians, and had spent all that she had, and was no better but rather grew worse. (Mark 5:26)

The woman has been desperate enough to "suffer much" under many different physicians. The Greek word used here, *pathousa*, indicates a deep and abiding suffering or a heavy emotion—perhaps recoiling at the things physicians did to her or the medicines they had her drink.

The religious authorities will say she holds some sin (as was the prevailing theory, echoed in Psalm 38 and Numbers 5:11-28), and that is why she is not well. Does she become scrupulous about her every thought and action? Does she feel small and insignificant? After all, she comes up behind Jesus in the crowd to touch him, then admits "in fear and trembling" that she touched him (Mark 5:33).

It could also be, according to the authorities, that it is not because of her sin but because of the sin of one of her parents that healing is denied. For that there is nothing she can do: no thought to retrieve, no action to recall, no penance to be done.

Perhaps the physicians knew she was desperate and preyed on that desperation. Regardless, now she is at the end of her financial wherewithal, and she is no better off than when she began. Indeed, the Gospel says, she "grew worse" with all those treatments (Mark 5:26). Twelve years of dashed hopes and increasing suffering.

> She had heard the reports about Jesus, and came up behind him in the crowd and touched his garment. For she said, "If I touch even his garments, I shall be made well." And immediately the hemorrhage ceased; and she felt in her body that she was healed of her disease. (Mark 5:27-29)

The woman turns to a man she has heard about, a man named Jesus—a healer from the town of Nazareth. She has nothing to lose and nothing left, and she believes, on the testimony of others, that he will heal her. She devises a plan to sneak up unnoticed and simply touch his cloak. She knows that will be enough to make her well.

And so it happens. The blood ceases to flow, and she knows she is healed.

Jesus meanwhile knows that *dunamis* has left him. The Greek word is most often translated as "power," but it also includes the ability to perform works of might, strength, force, or energy.

In this rare case, Jesus does not know whom he has healed. Perhaps he knows that someone was afraid to come forward yet desperate enough to risk attention. He looks for this person, searching the crowd to see who is changed. He doesn't look in anger but with compassion. "Daughter," he whispers as the woman comes forth "in fear and trembling," falling down before him (Mark 5:34, 33).

She is afraid. All these people press in on him, none of whom she should be in contact with, as the Levitical purity laws insist. What will they do to her when they see it is the hemorrhaging woman? Will they throw stones? What will Jesus say as she throws herself at his feet? She fears a rebuke.

But it is not. "Daughter, your faith has made you well; go in peace, and be healed of your disease" (Mark 5:34).

In his presence, she is healed—and loved.

Application: Apply What You Learned

We all long to be in the presence of others—to have authentic friendships, relationships in which we are free to laugh, love, and share. We, like the hemorrhaging woman, need to feel that we belong somewhere. Like her, we may go to great lengths and endure many trials to be in relationships. Yet the time, emotion, and money we spend looking for cures for our loneliness often leave us no better and growing worse.

Our afflictions can hold us in isolation. The threat of germs or viral infections that would derail a healing process is a very present concern for some. The weight of isolation coupled with degrading medical treatments leave us fearful of others. We don't want friends to encounter us in our state of physical disarray. We are embarrassed by our imperfections and our daily struggles to complete mundane tasks.

The same may hold true when we are in emotional or spiritual disarray—when life isn't going the way we planned. A separation, a divorce, a sudden death, a mental illness, a wayward and hurting child, a job loss: any of these events can leave us wounded and vulnerable. We hide from others, feeling as though we need to have it all together. We decline dinner invitations, we worry about what others might say about us, and we avoid the looks of pity.

We think ourselves unlovable and unseeable. This is not true, Jesus tells us.

The hemorrhaging woman took a risk in entering the crowd, letting her blood-stained clothing identify her. Once healed, she fell at Jesus' feet in fear and trembling, knowing the power he truly had. He who had the power to restore her also could identify her by her disease, she knew. But he did not send her away or create a scene. Instead he called her "Daughter" and welcomed her into his presence.

In one of the great paradoxes of life, we form friendships and create communities but also isolate others. We sometimes stand with the righteous townsfolk. We isolate others because we are afraid of their "unclean" ideas. We are uncomfortable around different thoughts, different cultures, and different ways of living. We think the solution to our discomfort is to keep our distance.

Like the remedies of those physicians who treated the hemorrhaging woman, our remedies can cause more pain. The divine physician has a different prescription: a prescription of presence.

The hemorrhaging woman heard about Jesus, and so have we. His is the great presence that animates our desires. His is the presence of love that drives our will. His is the healing presence that soothes our wounds.

"If I touch even his garments, I shall be made well," we can say (Mark 5:28). The presence of the Lord is the place of all healing. We can sit before him and even abide with him in the Eucharist. We can speak to him about our isolation, our infirmities, our heartaches. He is the author of our healing.

𝒫ractical: Take Action

The basis for Jesus' great commandment, "Love one another as I have loved you" (John 15:12), isn't merely a casual decree to do-what-Jesus-did, but to encounter the presence of Jesus in others and to see others as Jesus sees them. Isolating others because of illness or injury, race or creed, or social gain or loss is not only detrimental to human flourishing, but it is damaging to our own social and spiritual health. We should, as Pope St. John Paul II tells us, "not be afraid," and be a healing presence to those who are suffering, struggling, and thinking they are alone in their pain.[5]

How can you receive this prescription of presence? Start your day in the presence of the Lord. Invite him to give your soul strength and clarity to animate the work of your day. Set your alarm for fifteen minutes earlier than you usually do. Many people prefer to pray early in the morning like this, before anything else can get in the way. If you are able, begin your prayer just before dawn. Or find a lovely image of the dawn that you can look at as you start your prayer time.

Start your day in the presence of the Lord.

Sit with your eyes closed, and envision the hemorrhaging woman's return to community life after Jesus heals her—a life with friends, a social circle, and most importantly, God. She has been brought out of isolation. This is God's will for you too.

Allow his presence to be with you, to fill you, to satisfy you, and to open your eyes to the community that he has given you. Consider how you can more fully participate in your community. Send a short note with a card to a suffering elderly person, letting them know that you are praying for their healing and strength; join a Bible study or healing prayer group; or serve in your local food pantry or homeless shelter. Thank God for his presence in your life and for leading you to full, wholehearted participation in your community.

CHAPTER SIX

The Wise and Foolish Bridesmaids

"Give us some of your oil, for our lamps are going out."
(Matthew 25:8)

"Then the kingdom of heaven shall be compared to ten maidens who took their lamps and went to meet the bridegroom. Five of them were foolish, and five were wise. For when the foolish took their lamps, they took no oil with them; but the wise took flasks of oil with their lamps. As the bridegroom was delayed, they all slumbered and slept. But at midnight there was a cry, 'Behold, the bridegroom! Come out to meet him.' Then all those maidens rose and trimmed their lamps. And the foolish said to the wise, 'Give us some of your oil, for our lamps are going out.' But the wise replied, 'Perhaps there will not be enough for us and for you; go rather to the dealers and buy for yourselves.' And while they went to buy, the bridegroom came, and those who were ready went in with him to the marriage feast; and the door was shut. Afterward the other maidens came also, saying, 'Lord, lord, open to us.' But he replied, 'Truly, I say to you, I do not know you.' Watch therefore, for you know neither the day nor the hour." (Matthew 25:1-13)

Scripture: Define the Passage

Another stitch too far from the last in a series of stitches too far from each other. Another imperfect tunic. Sigh.

It seemed to the young woman that her hems were always a tad uneven, her garments a little tight across the shoulders or loose around the waist. Her pieces looked lovely from the outside, and she received many compliments on her needlework. Only a distinguishing eye would notice the flaws. But she, like her father, had a very distinguishing eye.

She picked up the beautiful linen mantle she had set aside earlier and slipped it on. She had spent weeks at the loom, weaving the dyed threads made of the finest flax in and out to create a stunning pattern. She received many compliments and offers of purchase, but she would not part with it—not because of emotional attachment but because she had been distracted for a moment and had woven a line of color incorrectly.

No one would notice, of course. The mistake was practically imperceptible. But she knew of the mantle's flaws and of her flaws.

It was the garment she had hoped to wear to the wedding celebration. Her father had offered her as a bridesmaid for the wedding, even before the exact day had been decided. That was their custom. The groom would fetch his bride at a time known only to him, his parents, and his groomsman.

Her father had spoken solemnly and in whispers about the groom. She knew that this man was important, perhaps the most important man of the chosen people. She was nervous in her role, feeling that perhaps she was not good enough, pretty enough, or talented enough to participate as one of the ten bridesmaids.

The groom would be dressed in his finest clothing and quite possibly exchange his traditional hat for a crown. He would gather his friends in the evening, and they would light candles and process through the town singing loudly. The intention was to alert the bride's father that the groom was on his way. The bride and her ten bridesmaids had to be at the ready upon his arrival.

Many townsfolk knew the anticipated day. However, that date came and went with no word from the groom.

Marriage ceremonies were very intimate rituals, this bridesmaid knew, as marriage was not only a union of families but a union of life. The husband and wife would come to know each other in a physical way, of course, but she thought it was the deep and abiding life together that was the greatest mystery. One would know all about the other person—their strengths and virtues as well as their weaknesses and vices. It was the latter that frightened her.

The thought that someone might know her flaws and see the uneven stitches of her life had kept her from chiding her father to find her a spouse. No, she thought, she would rather be alone with her imperfections than let the world know her inadequacies.

Her thoughts were interrupted by the shouts in the streets. The mysterious bridegroom had come after all. She smiled at her timing, as she was already dressed. She grabbed her lamp and headed for the rendezvous area with the other girls her age. There she looked down at her attire. In the dark, with only her lamp burning, she could still see the mistake in her pattern. So bold. So blaring. So obvious. Everyone must see it.

She shifted the lamp a bit, to no avail. All she could see was the error in the weave. And then there was the other error, the error in judgment.

In her haste and her focus on the mantle's imperfections, she had forgotten the extra flask of oil. She would have to run and get one. Yes, the groom might come while she was away, but it would be fine. He would not want to be seen with an imperfect girl like her anyway.

Observe: Discover the Message

In the Jewish wedding customs of this time, the parents arranged for the joining of two families, although the potential bride and groom often had a voice. The man proposed to his bride over a glass of wine, and she formally agreed by sharing the cup with him. He then returned home to build the bridal chamber and home, often an addition to his family's home. In the meantime, the woman readied her trousseau and chose her bridesmaids.

The bride then waited, with her veil and lamp at her bedside, for her betrothed to collect her from her parents' home. She knew he would come in the dark of night, with an entourage carrying candles, blowing a *shofar*, and perhaps singing the words of Solomon:

> Behold, you are beautiful, my love,
> behold, you are beautiful! . . .
> You are all fair, my love;
>   there is no flaw in you. . . .
>   you have ravished my heart with a glance of your
>   eyes. (Song of Solomon 4:1, 7, 9)

This serenade was not only for the bride but for the villagers to hear as well. The entire community must know that he had chosen her above all others.

> "Ten maidens . . . took their lamps and went to meet the bridegroom." (Matthew 25:1)

The bridesmaids helped the bride prepare for her new life and waited at the home with her. They shared in the tasks that a bride needed to accomplish, baking and sewing and preparing for the day. They too kept their wedding clothing and lamps at the ready. They shared in the bride's joy and excitement and acted as lookouts for the groom and his men.

The unique role of the bridesmaids, somewhat lost in the modern wedding ceremony, was to escort the groom to his bride. The bridesmaids joined the wedding party outside the home, standing beside the groomsmen. The groom then left his own men, stood amid the bridesmaids, and let them guide him to where his bride was waiting.

> "When the foolish took their lamps, they took no oil with them; but the wise took flasks of oil with their lamps. As the bridegroom was delayed, they all slumbered and slept." (Matthew 25:3-5)

In this parable, the bridesmaids are waiting with their bride. But the groom and his men are delayed, and the bridesmaids become drowsy and fall asleep. At midnight there is a shout, "Behold, the bridegroom! Come out to meet him" (Matthew 25:6) At the darkest hour of night, the bridegroom approaches in light and with song. There is recognition and movement and the relighting of lamps. The groom is coming to collect his bride!

Alas, as with many weddings, there is drama. Amid the joy and the commotion, half of the bridesmaids have neglected to bring their flasks of oil, and they *think* their light will not last. Our bridesmaid in the story above is one of those young women.

> "The foolish said to the wise, 'Give us some of your oil, for our lamps are going out.' But the wise replied, 'Perhaps there will not be enough for us and for you; go rather to the dealers and buy for yourselves.'" (Matthew 25:8-9)

The wise will not share. They know that their oil is not enough for the others; it is meant only for them. In wanting to help, they suggest to the five that they leave their posts and head into town, where they might find what they are looking for.

> "And while they went to buy, the bridegroom came, and those who were ready went in with him to the marriage feast; and the door was shut. Afterward the other maidens came also, saying, 'Lord, lord, open to us.'" (Matthew 25:10-11)

The foolish go in haste to make their purchase. While they are away, the groom joyously arrives, taking the five waiting bridesmaids inside, where they lead him to his bride. As they enter, the door locks behind them, and the wedding festivities begin. The other maidens return, having purchased what they think they need, and ask for admittance. But the bridegroom says to them, "Truly, I say to you, I do not know you" (Matthew 25:12).

The parable ends with a moral: "Watch therefore, for you know neither the day nor the hour" (Matthew 25:13).

Application: Apply What You Learned

Have you ever wondered why the wise did not share with the foolish? After all, sharing is the Christian way, isn't it? Love your enemies. Bless those who curse you. Offer the other cheek. Give away your coat and your shirt as well.

Don't expect those necessities to be returned either. And on top of it all, do not judge others while you're changing the world (see Luke 6:27-37).

Why wouldn't the wise bridesmaids share their oil if they were so wise? This parable has nothing to do with sharing and everything to do with being. The Greek text translated literally would read thus: "Give us of the oil of you, for the lamps of us are going out" (Matthew 25:8). Ponder that for a moment. Meditate on the "oil of you" and the "going out."

It seems as though each individual bridesmaid has oil meant for her and no one else. Notice too that the lamps of the foolish aren't out yet, but the women *believe* they will go out before the bridegroom appears. How might we apply these words and thoughts to our lives?

Imagine that you are a bridesmaid waiting for the Lord to come. You have your purified oil, but it is swirled with imperfections. You think you need to be perfect for anyone, including the Lord, to love you.

You foolishly believe that you are not good enough.

You foolishly believe that you are not beautiful enough.

You foolishly believe that you are not lovable enough.

You foolishly believe that you are not enough.

You *think* your oil will run out. You *think* you need to go elsewhere to get what you need to meet your Beloved.

This parable is about standing before the Lord exactly as you are, with whatever oil is in your lamp. For the Lord knows you intimately, as Jeremiah reminds us:

Before I formed you in the womb I knew you,
and before you were born I consecrated you.
(Jeremiah 1:5)

You—exactly as you are, wonderfully and beautifully made. Nothing in you is hidden, and nothing in you is perfect. Our Lord understands your imperfections, having taken the essence of human nature to himself. Yet he still craves an intimate relationship with you.

> *Our Lord understands your imperfections, yet he still craves an intimate relationship with you.*

Why might the bridegroom fail to recognize the maidens who went off to fill their lamps? Because they went into the world and filled their lamps with oil from the marketplace, instead of waiting for the bridegroom to supply what they lacked. You see, we who struggle for perfection try to fill our lamps with oil that is not meant for us.

It's true that we look to other women, who have our best interests at heart, for guidance. This is what friendship is all about. Wise women know, however, that what makes *others'* lights shine can't make *them* shine. They understand human nature and God's providence and plan for each person. That is why they are wise and why we seek them out.

Still, they agonize with us and offer suggestions. Try this. Go here. Do that. They want us to be calm and whole and healed as soon as possible. There is a sense of urgency in their advice, as they want us to stand beside them and meet the Bridegroom when he arrives.

So we fill our lamps with oil that makes us unrecognizable. We fill them with lies and half-truths and unhelpful hints. We cheapen ourselves by trying to be what the world wants us to be or look how the world wants us to look. We believe the lie that our imperfections make us unlovable, and we act accordingly. Like the foolish virgins who stood outside the door after filling their lamps with the crude oil of the world, we become someone the Lord doesn't recognize. How foolish we can be!

The Lord loves you just the way you are, with all your imperfections and your flaws and your murky oil, iridescent with experience.

The wise bridesmaids are imperfect too. They bring everything they have and all that they are, and they wait for the Lord to bring them into the wedding banquet. From their flasks of inadequacy, they pour what oil they have into their lamps, to light them for the Lord. They stand holding their wounds and their scars in their vulnerability and let the Lord take them as they are.

Jesus desires our presence in the kingdom, regardless of when that day may come. He desires us the way a husband loves and desires his beloved on their wedding day. Our relationship with him is one of intimacy—physical, emotional, social, and spiritual. Jesus' deep and abiding love permeates every aspect of our lives. This is the reason he chooses the analogy of a wedding to talk about our life with him beyond this earthly veil.

Practical: Take Action

Like the bridesmaids who were unrecognizable to the Lord, the way we see our imperfections isn't always recognizable to others either. When we stand before the Lord, knocking at his door, he will look deep into our eyes and pierce our hearts. He will know how much we love him, and then how we loved others as he loved us. He will see us as a bridegroom sees his bride, overlooking our flaws and imperfections. He will see us through the eyes of love and find that even with our imperfections, we are perfectly amazing.

How do I accept my imperfections? Two tendencies can turn a desire to be a perfect disciple of Christ into perfectionism: pride and scrupulosity. Like our bridesmaid whose flask was running low, we may want to hide the flaws in our work (pride) or take every flaw and put it under a microscope (scrupulosity).

Pride prevents grace from entering our lives, while scrupulosity distorts our flaws and makes our imperfections larger than life. As St. Catherine of Siena is credited with saying, "Be who God meant you to be and you will set the world on fire."

Take some time to journal as you reflect on these questions:

- Who did God create you to be? Are you trying to be someone you are not?

- What are the characteristics of the oil God intended for your flask?

- If you are struggling with the not-good-enough associated with scrupulosity, reflect on the Samaritan woman at the well and her encounter with Jesus (John 4:4-44) and answer the question, Why did Jesus choose this woman to reveal his identity, knowing her many flaws?

- If you are weighted by pride, ponder the humility of Mary, the mother of God (Luke 1:46-48) and ask yourself, How can I practice humility in my day?

- If you are struggling with self-image, reflect on God's love for you (Psalm 139:13-14) and write down the ways in which you are "wonderfully made."

CHAPTER SEVEN

The Woman with the Alabaster Jar

Standing behind him at his feet, weeping, she began to wet his feet with her tears, and wiped them with the hair of her head, and kissed his feet, and anointed them with the ointment. (Luke 7:38)

One of the Pharisees asked him to eat with him, and he went into the Pharisee's house, and sat at table. And behold, a woman of the city, who was a sinner, when she learned that he was sitting at table in the Pharisee's house, brought an alabaster flask of ointment, and standing behind him at his feet, weeping, she began to wet his feet with her tears, and wiped them with the hair of her head, and kissed his feet, and anointed them with the ointment. Now when the Pharisee who had invited him saw it, he said to himself, "If this man were a prophet, he would have known who and what sort of woman this is who is touching him, for she is a sinner." And Jesus answering said to him, "Simon, I have something to say to you." And he answered, "What is it, Teacher?" "A certain creditor had two debtors; one owed five hundred denarii, and the other fifty. When they could not pay, he forgave them both. Now which of them will love him more?" Simon answered, "The one, I suppose, to whom he forgave more." And he said to him, "You have judged rightly." Then turning toward the woman he said to Simon, "Do you see this woman? I entered your house, you gave me no water for my feet, but she has wet my feet with her tears and wiped them with her hair. You gave me no kiss, but from the time I came in she has not ceased to kiss my feet. You did not anoint my head with oil, but she has anointed my feet with ointment. Therefore I tell you, her sins, which are many, are forgiven, for she loved much; but he who is forgiven little, loves little." And he said to her, "Your sins are forgiven." Then those who were at table with him began to say among themselves, "Who is this, who even forgives sins?" And he said to the woman, "Your faith has saved you; go in peace." (Luke 7:36-50)

Scripture: Define the Passage

"Have you seen that woman?" the Temple guard asks. "You know, that sinner woman. I need her for an evening—for me and my friends."

She knows they are looking for her. She wonders how much longer she can keep to the shadows. It's a big city, but there aren't many places to hide. Maybe, she thinks, it's time to step into the light. It's time to put the past behind her. But it's the kind of past that whispers to her heart that she will never be respected by other women, find a husband to protect and love her, or have children to be proud of.

She wants to be a part of a family. She wants to give and receive the kind of love that has strength and depth—the kind of love that protects her future and forgives her past, one that cherishes and sustains, one that endures, one that makes her feel beloved so that she can give the same love in return. She longs for an extravagant and radical love.

This woman knows that others talk about her, judge her, keep their children away from her. She has been abandoned by those who should have taken care of her.

And yet, if she reaches back in her faded memories, she remembers the gentle voice of her father and the laughter of her mother. She finds herself, a small slip of a girl, at the Friday *Shabbat* table. She and her brothers have washed the dust from their feet and the dirt off their faces. They work the land, and her role is to spread feed and carry water buckets.

In her memory of this night, she watches her mother set the table. Her father sits down at one end of the table, and her mother at the other. Her three brothers take their places. As dusk falls, so do their heads in prayer. Her mother lights the candles. Her father begins, "Hear O Israel, the Lord your God is one."

Her father smiles upon her, as he always does, saying the blessing for daughters. She watches her brothers' solemn faces as they receive the blessing for sons. He pours the wine into the cup.

The cup was a wedding gift, signifying the impossible love of a man for a woman beneath him in status but above him in kindness, gentleness, honesty, and beauty. In this memory, the grown-up little girl now feels this extravagant love: the love of God, who will send a redeemer; the love her father had for her mother; the love her elder brothers had for her. She is enveloped in that evening's glow, and for a moment, she forgets where she is now, what she has done, and where she is hiding.

"Have you seen the sinner woman?" The guard's question brings her back to reality, the one that finds her hiding in the shadows, full of angry pride and broken promises.

She has heard of the man Jesus. Hiding behind an olive tree once in Capernaum, she listened to him preaching. He chastised the scribes. She moved closer. He condemned the Pharisees. She leaned in. He blessed the poor. She took a step. He came for the sinner. She came out of the shadows. He looked her straight in the eye. Her heart exploded, and her feet took flight.

Returning home, she sat in the dark thinking about her newfound joy and pondering her next move. This man loved her, all of her, abundantly. She felt it in his momentary gaze. She *knew* it deep in her soul. His presence reminded her of the *Shabbat* table of her memories, the one set in innocence and filled with love.

What would she do now? One of the many skills she had learned in the shadows was to think clearly.

A few days later, she heard the news that he was making his way to Nain. He would be at Simon's *Shabbat* table this evening. She began planning.

She went to her hiding place and dug up the coins she had been saving to start a new life in another town. This

Jesus had given her new ideas to ponder. The perfumer looked at her suspiciously as she entered with an alabaster jar, but she didn't care. Carefully she poured the ointment into the jar, then made her way to Simon's house under cover of darkness.

Getting into the house was easy. She had a talent and a reputation at gatherings; men opened doors for her that were closed to most women. She spotted Jesus at the head of the table and noticed his dirty feet. How could Simon not offer him the most basic of hospitality?

She could do for him what Simon would not. She would give him her heart and her soul. She would love him as only a redeemed woman could, regardless of what anyone else would say. Extravagantly, recklessly, with abandon.

She stood behind him, and then the tears came. She began to bathe his feet with her tears and to dry them with her hair. She kissed those feet, then brought out the ointment. She sensed the eyes of the elite upon her, but she didn't care. Jesus was her focus.

Observe: Discover the Message

> One of the Pharisees asked him to eat with him, and he went into the Pharisee's house, and sat at table. (Luke 7:36)

Jesus has healed the sick and raised the dead, and word is spreading that he is a miracle worker. Everyone wants to be near him, and great crowds follow him.

Simon the Pharisee must know of the prophecies about the Messiah, for his job is to comb the sacred Scriptures and comment on them. Perhaps he wonders if this is the One for whom he's been waiting.

The Pharisees are a powerful group. They might think that God would choose the Messiah from among them, the "separated ones." They are not enamored of Jesus. Perhaps Simon has second thoughts about inviting this rebel teacher and some friends to dine with him. What of his reputation and political agenda? Still, Simon is interested and curious. And Jesus has a large following, which might be to Simon's advantage.

Notice that Simon doesn't extend to Jesus the rituals due an honored guest. There is no kiss of welcome, no gentle rinsing of worn and dusty feet. This could be interpreted by the other guests as a not-so-subtle rebuke. Those who are interested in what Jesus has to say might hope the invitation is an act of reconciliation on the part of Jewish leaders.

Maybe Simon hopes to deftly please all. It is politics as usual. These Jewish leaders profess a mutual love and respect, but it is not clear if they are sincere.

> And behold, a woman of the city, who was a sinner, when she learned that he was sitting at table in the Pharisee's house, brought an alabaster flask of ointment. (Luke 7:37)

In most homes, tables were low to the floor, and food was eaten while sitting on thin pillows or cushions. It might be possible, in the home of Simon the Pharisee, a man of wealth, that Jesus is sitting on a small sofa with his legs stretched out. It is a small and intimate setting—only Simon, Jesus, and a few other Jewish men, in addition to the attendants who are serving. Our woman enters this room of important men carrying her alabaster jar of ointment.

Alabaster (*alabastron*) is a stone often used in making perfume bottles. These bottles had very long necks, to prevent the ointment from spilling or evaporating. A host would break the neck of a jar and let the aroma flood the space as he anointed his honored guest. It was an expensive ritual. Neither the jar nor the ointment could be used again.

These jars and their ointment were often broken and spilled at the death of a beloved one. The woman's alabaster jar was purchased at no small price, a sacrifice on her part.

The Greek word for "ointment" is *muron*. It was a liquid salve made of olive oil and spices. The word is also translated as "perfume," since the smell was pleasant and powerful. The word has a foreign counterpart: myrrh, the gift bestowed upon Jesus at his birth (see Matthew 2:11).

As valuable as the alabaster jar was, the *muron* was more so. Together, the words "alabaster jar of ointment" are synonymous with extravagant love.

> Standing behind him at his feet, weeping, she began
> to wet his feet with her tears, and wiped them with
> the hair of her head, and kissed his feet, and anointed
> them with the ointment. (Luke 7:38)

Our woman of the city kneels at the feet of Jesus, weeping. Her tears fall like rain, bathing his feet, washing off the dust. Her hair, like her soul, has come undone. She uses it to dry his feet, kissing them while doing so.

Simon looks at Jesus, while Jesus looks into Simon.

Jesus watches her, in all humility and love, eyes shining, heart expanding. Simon is perhaps stunned to silence by both the audacity of the woman who walks into his home uninvited and this man who allows her to touch him.

> Now when the Pharisee who had invited him saw
> it, he said to himself, "If this man were a prophet, he
> would have known who and what sort of woman this
> is who is touching him, for she is a sinner." And Jesus
> answering said to him, "Simon, I have something to
> say to you." (Luke 7:39-40)

Simon looks *at* Jesus, while Jesus looks *into* Simon. And Jesus finds something that needs a gentle correction. He instructs Simon on the meaning of love.

Jesus recounts the story of the creditor who canceled debts; one debtor owed much, and one owed little. Jesus asks Simon, "Which of them will love him more?" (Luke 7:42).

Notice that Jesus doesn't use the language of commerce or business or law. He doesn't say which of the debtors would respect the creditor more or which one would find the creditor more powerful or forgiving or honorable. No. He asks Simon which one will *love* the creditor more. Jesus is asking Simon—and everyone else in the room— to leave politics, business, and reputation aside. He opens their eyes to the power and primacy of God's abundant and radical love.

> Then turning toward the woman he said to Simon, "Do you see this woman? I entered your house, you gave me no water for my feet, but she has wet my feet with her tears and wiped them with her hair. You gave me no kiss, but from the time I came in she has not ceased to kiss my feet. You did not anoint my head with oil, but she has anointed my feet with ointment." (Luke 7:44-46)

A room full of people are watching this play out. Jesus speaks aloud what everyone already knows. Simon did not greet his guest with the traditional kiss of peace, and he neglected to offer water for feet washing. Nor did he offer to anoint this one who is obviously a man of God, for everyone present has seen and heard what Jesus has done.

Finally, to our woman with the broken alabaster jar, who has given Jesus her tears, her meager wealth, and her love, he acknowledges his love in return.

"Your sins are forgiven. . . . Your faith has saved you; go in peace." (Luke 7:48, 50)

God is a God of extravagant love.

*A*pplication: Apply What You Learned

English can be a poor language for conveying expressions and their meaning. We "love" coffee, ice cream, a significant other, our pet, and the warmth of the sun in the deep freeze of winter.

In the Hebrew language of the Jews, there are two words for "love." The first and highest love is that between the Creator and the created. It is the covenantal word *chesed*. It is a marital word, denoting steadfastness, binding, and abiding. It is an emotional word, evoking a deep longing for and union with the other. It is long-suffering, hope filled, and ever present.

Chesed contains the language of law in words like justice, power, and obedience. It is imbued with friendship, kindness, mercy, and truth. It conveys deep affection, especially for the lowly and oppressed. It is a word that increases the spiritual life, offering redemption and forgiveness. It is the key to the preservation of life. It is the defining word of the relationship between the Lord and the chosen people.

The second word for love is *ahava*. This type of love is marital also; in fact, it is primarily defined as the union of a man and a woman that begets children. It is affectionate and intimate, with a deep undercurrent of friendship. It is based on outward action.

Ahava is also a word of great longing. One gives the gift of time with great devotion, regardless of what one might receive in return. *Ahava*, like *chesed*, is a verb. Jacob *ahava* Rachel, David *ahava* Bathsheba, Solomon *ahava* his foreign wives. It might be what a couple in an arranged marriage came to feel for each other.

Not to be outdone, Greek has four expressions for love. *Eros* is generally considered the lowest of all loves. It is the base sexual attraction that we have for another human being. It's highly erotic and passionate. It evokes a racing of the heart and an overwhelming desire for touch and physical union. It's the longing for physical intimacy that we know as infatuation. While it is often the point of entry into a new relationship, it's also temporary, as it's based on sometimes tumultuous feelings of physical desire. Once satiated, this desire often abates. It may or may not be part of a long-term relationship.

Another love is *phileo*—a fondness or affection for friends and community, based on our common interests. It's what you feel during an evening out with old college friends, catching up over a shared bottle of wine and a cheese-and-fruit platter. Or during your book club meeting, when someone shares intimate details related to a book's content. Or when dissecting a thought-provoking play with friends over dinner. *Phileo* involves deep emotion.

A third type of Greek love is *storge*, a familial form of affection. It's the love we have for our parents and close relatives. It has a sense of obligation and longevity and struggle. It's sometimes difficult, as you do not get to choose whom to love here. You might not even like a family member, but you are beholden to love them. An uncle who is snarky, an aunt who is critical, or a cousin who is combative all live in this type of love.

Sometimes parental love falls here, as when an adult child makes choices a parent vehemently disagrees with. We love family members regardless of their mistakes and errors in judgment.

The highest love is *agape*, the gift of self, total self—mind, body, soul, spirit. *Agape* embraces everything: the good, the bad, the everyday. It is the kind of love that Paul speaks about to the good folks of Corinth:

> Love is patient and kind; love is not jealous or boastful; it is not arrogant or rude. Love does not insist on its own way; it is not irritable or resentful; it does not rejoice at wrong, but rejoices in the right. Love bears all things, believes all things, hopes all things, endures all things. (1 Corinthians 13:4-7)

Nothing is hidden, and nothing is unsaid with *agape*. It is unconditional, sacrificial, complete, timeless, unending.

When Jesus says to Simon, "Therefore I tell you, her sins, which are many, are forgiven, for she loved much" (Luke 7:47), he speaks of this kind of extravagant love. And Simon knows it.

This woman of the city, a sinner, brings herself to the Lord. Her sins, her reputation, her entire self—she literally lays all at his feet. She is vulnerable. She hides nothing. She gives what little she has, regardless of what anyone thinks. She loves with reckless abandon. *Chesed, avaha,* and *agape* love in action.

In our modern-day reading, we might miss the depth of this woman's reckless love. She enters a room full of men and allows her long hair to cascade around her. This is scandalous behavior, inappropriate and maybe punishable. Although not based in law, the common practice was for women to keep their heads covered and hair unseen.

This woman gives what little she has, regardless of what anyone thinks. She loves with reckless abandon.

Jesus must know this, and yet he does not correct her behavior. He rather approves of this radical demonstration of love, even using it as an entry point to chiding Simon. This is the way authentic love should be, he says. It is a radical love that isn't self-centered, sealed by social acceptance, or self-enclosed.

Jesus wants us to break open our alabaster jars.

Practical: Take Action

Agape love is risky business. Risk involves value, impact, and vulnerability. We weigh our value, asses our impact, and determine our levels of openness. It is an exposure to danger, suffering, and uncertainty. Of those three, it is never a question of *if*; it is always a statement of *how much*. Risk measures costs and benefits, and the threat of collateral damage is inherent. In love, we often look at the scales to see if the sides are even, and if they are not, then we refuse to love with the reckless abandon of our woman in a room full of men judging her every action. We forget how Jesus sees every single woman, through *agape* eyes.

How can I live my life with authentic love at its core, seeing with *agape* eyes? Reach out to someone whose company you don't always enjoy and who is undergoing a difficult time. Invite them to tell their story, and listen with an open heart. Or spend time at a homeless shelter, food shelf, thrift store, or home for the dying. Resist the urge to make a food, clothing, or monetary donation, and instead, give the gift of your time and presence.

Or you might encourage a friend, coworker, or acquaintance who is struggling. Invite them to breakfast, coffee, or another outing that they would enjoy. Ask the Lord to show you how else you might be able to help her. She might need a listening ear, or maybe a specific gift or act of service will lift her burden. Maybe she would appreciate an invitation to join you for Mass or to pray together regularly.

A small act, done with love, can set someone's life on a trajectory of hope. Thank the Lord for allowing you to be present to this person. Ask Jesus for the grace to be ever more willing to take risks in loving others and being available to them.

CHAPTER EIGHT

Elizabeth

"Why is this granted me, that the
mother of my Lord should come to
me?" (Luke 1:43)

In the days of Herod, king of Judea, there was a priest named Zechariah, of the division of Abijah; and he had a wife of the daughters of Aaron, and her name was Elizabeth. And they were both righteous before God, walking in all the commandments and ordinances of the Lord blameless. But they had no child, because Elizabeth was barren, and both were advanced in years.

Now while he was serving as priest before God when his division was on duty, according to the custom of the priesthood, it fell to him by lot to enter the temple of the Lord and burn incense. And the whole multitude of the people were praying outside at the hour of incense. And there appeared to him an angel of the Lord standing on the right side of the altar of incense. And Zechariah was troubled when he saw him, and fear fell upon him. But the angel said to him, "Do not be afraid, Zechariah, for your prayer is heard, and your wife Elizabeth will bear you a son, and you shall call his name John. . . .

And Zechariah said to the angel, "How shall I know this? For I am an old man, and my wife is advanced in years." And the angel answered him, "I am Gabriel, who stand in the presence of God; and I was sent to speak to you, and to bring you this good news. And behold, you will be silent and unable to speak until the day that these things come to pass, because you did not believe my words, which will be fulfilled in their time." And the people were waiting for Zechariah, and they wondered at his delay in the temple. And when he came out, he could not speak to them, and they perceived that he had seen a vision in the temple; and he made signs to them and remained dumb. And when his time of service was ended, he went to his home.

After these days his wife Elizabeth conceived, and for five months she hid herself, saying, "Thus the Lord has done to me in the days when he looked on me, to take away my reproach among men." . . .

[The angel said to Mary,] "And behold, your kinswoman Elizabeth in her old age has also conceived a son; and this is the sixth month with her who was called barren. For with God nothing will be impossible." . . .

In those days Mary arose and went with haste into the hill country, to a city of Judah, and she entered the house of Zechariah and greeted Elizabeth. And when Elizabeth heard the greeting of Mary, the babe leaped in her womb; and Elizabeth was filled with the Holy Spirit and she exclaimed with a loud cry, "Blessed are you among women, and blessed is the fruit of your womb! And why is this granted me, that the mother of my Lord should come to me? For behold, when the voice of your greeting came to my ears, the babe in my womb leaped for joy. And blessed is she who believed that there would be a fulfilment of what was spoken to her from the Lord." (Luke 1:5-13, 18-25, 36-37, 39-45)

Scripture: Define the Passage

Sitting beneath the olive tree, she looked down at her sun-kissed hands to see a new line of longevity and a faint shade of age, and she wondered when those appeared. Although she was "getting on in years," as she heard the maidens whisper, she didn't feel old—or look particularly old, for that matter. Her body was lean and firm from helping her husband with home repairs and carrying water to and from the well. Her skin was still soft and supple, for the most part, as she took care of her appearance by using aloe and herbs grown in her garden.

When traders wandered through their small village on the way to somewhere important, Zechariah occasionally bought her salt for food, a token of his admiration for her cooking skills, but also bath salts, a token of his love for her. He liked to compare her to Abraham's wife,

Sarah, as she aged slowly and gracefully. This "getting on in years" wasn't so bad.

Elizabeth smiled at the thought of her prayer life. It was generally rich and full and vibrant, despite the unanswered petition for a child. She was a woman of hope and endurance, a true daughter in the line of Aaron. These characteristics brought Zechariah to her; as a priest in the line of Abijah, she was the spiritual wife he needed.

Each morning Elizabeth and Zechariah came to the table to prepare their hearts for the day ahead. She would set the table and light a candle, and together they would offer their quiet thanksgivings and petitions to the Lord. This was not a required custom among their people, but they had settled into the habit at the beginning of their marriage.

Each Friday at sunset, they would light two candles, with a glass of wine and two loaves of *challah* bread at hand, and begin their prayers. Zechariah recited the *Kiddush* prayer, omitting the traditional blessing of children. Each *Shabbat* was a reminder of their longing.

The petition for a child was the first prayer of the morning, the unspoken prayer of their hearts throughout the day, and the last prayer of the evening. Zechariah had told Elizabeth that when it was his turn to serve as priest and burn the incense in the temple of the Lord, he would pray for her reproach to be taken from her and for her to conceive a son. Even after all these years, he still prayed for her.

Zechariah loved Elizabeth. She wondered if he knew when they got married how difficult their lives would be.

She had imagined a life abundant with children and knew her husband had thought the same way. Over the course of the years, he came to love her not for what she could or could not do for him but for who she was.

Her lack of children, Elizabeth thought, was why the people of the village sometimes avoided her. She wasn't the only one who felt the sting. Zechariah too was sometimes excluded from gatherings and events of the men.

Elizabeth trusted in Yahweh's plan for her and Zechariah, though it was a mystery to her. She knew that God's "way is perfect" and that "the promise of LORD proves true" (Psalm 18:30).

Elizabeth looked up from the shade of the olive tree and saw her husband returning from his time of service. He walked quickly toward her, a confused look in his eyes but a wry smile on his face. He looked somehow different, she thought. Still she was delighted to see him and welcomed him with open arms.

Observe: Discover the Message

> In the days of Herod, king of Judea, there was a priest named Zechariah, of the division of Abijah; and he had a wife of the daughters of Aaron, and her name was Elizabeth. (Luke 1:5)

Names are important in the Hebrew tradition, just as they are for us. We sometimes wrestle with a variety of names before choosing just the *right* one for our children. On ordination, clergy add the name "Father" or "Deacon" or "Bishop" in front of their given names. Consecrated religious often choose a new name, perhaps that of a saint for whom they have a special affection.

The Hebrew name "Elizabeth" is taken from two words: *'el*, meaning "God," and *shaba*, "to swear." Our heroine's name is often translated as "God is my oath." But *shaba* is also the number seven in Hebrew, a number of perfection. It is associated with abundance and plenty, so we get the other meanings of Elizabeth, "God is bountiful" or "God is plentiful."

Elizabeth is a woman of great promise. She is of the lineage of Aaron, a respected and treasured elder of the chosen people. She is an honest and upright woman, a righteous woman before God. She obeys the commandments of the Lord blamelessly, loving the Lord with all her heart, all her soul, all her mind, and all her strength (see Deuteronomy 6:5). She loves her neighbor as herself (Leviticus 19:18). She is a woman of exceptional character and abiding holiness.

Zechariah is no different. He is a man of exceptional character and abiding holiness. His name is from two Hebrew words, *zakhar*, meaning "to remember," and *yah*, referring to Yahweh. Therefore "Zechariah" means "God remembers."

Zechariah is of the Levite priestly clan, which originated at the time of Moses. Zechariah must ponder this lineage from time to time. Everything in his life with Elizabeth would indicate abundant blessings.

> They were both righteous before God, walking in all the commandments and ordinances of the Lord blameless. But they had no child, because Elizabeth was barren, and both were advanced in years. (Luke 1:6-7)

Elizabeth and Zechariah seem to have everything on their side for a fruitful marriage, but they have one gaping and very public failure. Elizabeth must wonder why this is so. Why her? Why does she carry this reproach wherever she goes? Zechariah too must wonder. Why him? Why do he and his beloved carry this stigma?

In Jewish law it was *possible* to divorce a wife for not producing a son, if the husband viewed this as an "indecency" (see Deuteronomy 24:1) and took the claim to a rabbi. Zechariah did not. He was willing to give up an heir and remain faithful to Elizabeth, despite the comments and the sideways glances that a

Elizabeth and Zechariah grew old together, living this paradox of a perfect life with unanswered prayers, shrouded in mystery.

barren couple would receive. They grew old together, living this paradox of a perfect life with unanswered prayers, shrouded in mystery.

> Now while he was serving as priest before God when his division was on duty, according to the custom of the priesthood, it fell to him by lot to enter the temple of the Lord and burn incense. . . . And there appeared to him an angel of the Lord standing on the right side of the altar of incense. (Luke 1:8-9, 11)

When Zechariah enters the Holy Place with the incense, to utter the prescribed prayers and the prayers of his heart, an angel of the Lord appears before him. The word "angel" in Hebrew is *mal'ach* and in Greek *ángelos*. Both mean "messenger," a bearer of news, good or bad. For Zechariah the news is good.

> "Your prayer is heard, and your wife Elizabeth will bear you a son, and you shall call his name John." (Luke 1:13)

This name is a mystery too. It is not the name of his father or the name of a male relative. It hardly seems like a Jewish name at all.

The longer Hebrew version of the name is Johanan, taken from the *ya* of the Lord's name and *hanan*, "to be gracious." Thus the name means "God is gracious." It is a mysterious name, yet apt for a child announced behind closed doors under cover of smoke and incense.

> Zechariah said to the angel, "How shall I know this? For I am an old man, and my wife is advanced in years." And the angel answered him, "I am Gabriel, who stand in the presence of God; and I was sent to speak to you, and to bring you this good news. And behold, you will be silent and unable to speak until the day that these things come to pass, because you did not believe my words, which will be fulfilled in their time." (Luke 1:18-20)

Zechariah is taken aback. *How can this be? I am an old man, as is my wife.* Both are beyond the age at which conception is a possibility.

But the angel answers, "I am Gabriel," meaning "man of God," and tells Elizabeth's husband of a punishment for his unbelief. Silence is a mysterious penance for a holy man whose work is to pray aloud in the temple.

> The people were waiting for Zechariah, and they wondered at his delay in the temple. And when he came out, he could not speak to them, and they perceived that he had seen a vision in the temple. (Luke 1:21-22)

When Zechariah finally leaves the Temple, he is not able to give the priestly blessing for which the men outside have been waiting. These men must be perplexed and in wonder. How did this happen? Why did this happen? Who did this?

They understand that Zechariah has seen a vision while in the Temple, but they do not know what it was or why it came to him. A mystery indeed.

> When his time of service was ended, he went to his home.
>   After these days his wife Elizabeth conceived, and for five months she hid herself, saying, "Thus the Lord has done to me in the days when he looked on me, to take away my reproach among men." (Luke 1:23-25)

Zechariah returns to his wife, and somehow he communicates to her what Gabriel predicted. Elizabeth does indeed conceive. She is incredibly grateful, praising the Lord for removing the disgrace of barrenness. Then she goes into seclusion for five months.

Surely the townspeople must notice. Where is the barren woman, and why is her husband mute? Has something happened?

While Elizabeth is in seclusion, the angel Gabriel goes to visit her young cousin Mary, to ask if she will be receptive to the Holy Spirit and allow God to take on human form in her womb. Mary gives her *fiat*, then sets out "with haste" to visit Elizabeth (Luke 1:39). Elizabeth's seclusion ends with Mary's arrival.

Mary is newly with child, probably not showing. But when Elizabeth sees Mary, she says, "Blessed are you among women, and blessed is the fruit of your womb! And why is this granted me, that the mother of my Lord should come to me?" (Luke 1:42-43).

$\mathcal{A}$pplication: Apply What You Learned

There is a difference between mystery and suspense, though we sometimes conflate the two. Suspense involves uncertainty, a feeling of anxiety or uneasiness or even dread. It includes some level of tension. Distrust, danger, and despair take our hands and clasp them tightly as we meander in the darkness. Emotions are on high alert. Fear lurks behind every choice. There is no obvious answer to our dilemma. Everything and anything are possible, and our mind races from one disastrous conclusion to another.

We say, "The suspense is killing me," and indeed it can. No one can live in a constant state of suspense.

Mystery, however, is where our faith lives and breathes. It assumes an underlying truth that once we reach the end of things, we will find clarity. Mystery has an aura of certainty, a hint of contentment, a suggestion of balance, trust, and order. There is a secret to uncover, to be sure, but the solution is ours to find, provided we are patient and follow the clues.

Contemplation is inherent to the process. The light of peace shows the way. Reason, discernment, and revelation are companions. Inspiration is our guide, and creativity the hand that helps the wrong turn become right. Hope is in the air. Living in mystery is woman fully alive.

We often find ourselves hiding in suspense when we should be living in mystery.

Elizabeth knows this. She prays with certainty that the Lord will hear her. She knows what she needs, and her desire is the prayer of her heart. It is a prayer for a son to love and to nurture, to take away her "reproach among men" (Luke 1:25). She is persistent in this prayer and shares it with her husband.

When Gabriel appears to Zechariah, he says, "Your prayer is heard" (Luke 1:13). This is the prayer of both him and his wife.

And perhaps it is the prayer of the people praying outside. After all, Elizabeth and Zechariah are preeminent members of their community, holy and righteous before God. A prayer request does not belong to you alone but to your posse, your tribe, your community in the Lord. St. Paul reminds us that "we, though many, are one body in Christ" (Romans 12:5), and this goes for prayer as well. The mystery is why we keep the desires of our hearts to ourselves when there is power in communal prayer.

Elizabeth awaits the answer to her prayer while in community, for the first words she utters upon finding herself with child are, "Thus the Lord has done to me in the days when he looked on me, to take away my reproach among men" (Luke 1:25). She certainly has friends in her community. She gathers water from the well with other women and meets them at the synagogue. She depends on them, and they depend on her, in both material and spiritual ways. Faith communities thrive with such mutual dependence and prayer. As Elizabeth waits for her prayers to be answered, so does her faith community.

Prayers are rarely answered the moment we lay them at the feet of the Lord. For Elizabeth it was a very long wait. It is in this waiting that we can be tempted to change the reel in our heads from mystery to suspense. We begin to doubt. We can lie awake at night, our personal prayers clutched to our chest in fear. Perhaps the fear is that someone may judge our state of holiness because our request has not yet been granted. Or that we will look foolish. Or that we are not good enough to be the recipient of an answer.

> Prayer should not be viewed from a vantage point of suspense but lived in the certainty of mystery that the Lord hears our prayers and will indeed give us an answer.

If that is you, head back to chapter 5 and look again at the woman healed of hemorrhage. Remember that prayer is a mystery worthy of the highest honor. It should not be viewed from a vantage point of suspense but lived in the certainty of mystery that the Lord hears our prayers and will indeed give us an answer.

God's bestowal of a child upon Elizabeth isn't just about the conception of a son; it is also about the removal of her disgrace and the bestowing of grace. That is how it is when God enters our lives. He takes away our brokenness and restores us to wholeness. We do not know when or why or even how, but we do know that it happens—miraculously or, should we say, mysteriously.

In Elizabeth's seclusion, she will spend quiet time nurturing her soul and the gratitude of her heart. She prepares for birth and motherhood: food and herbs are gathered and eaten for strength, birthing material and swaddling cloths are made for the delivery, prayers are learned, and animals are provided for the ritual purification and presentation (see Leviticus 12:6-8).

Elizabeth has likely seen many births, but she is advanced in years and does not know what to expect. She is only grateful for this gift of life that her God has given. And so she nurtures both her soul and this child, unseen to the world at large. This is the way of mystery, nurturing gratitude for what is present as we prepare in hope for the future that unfolds.

Elizabeth and Mary meet, and the spiritual world explodes. Out of the deep desire of Elizabeth's heart comes something she could not have foreseen: her son will be the forerunner of the Messiah. Here we see a mystery of God. While we think our prayer may be for our own need or good, God can put a desire inside us for a reason. Often our prayer is part of something larger than we can see, a plan more perfect than we can imagine, a path resplendent with beauty and grace. Elizabeth's prayer was actually for the world, and she had no idea.

Elizabeth asks, "Why is this granted me, that the mother of my Lord should come to me?" (Luke 1:43). Elizabeth has felt her child leap in the womb, and she knows that the life of that child and the life of Mary's child will be forever linked. She is filled with wisdom, a gift of the Holy Spirit, for she knows that her cousin carries the Christ child. Her proclamation of this truth is the first recorded, and it is for all the world to know.

In the quiet of Elizabeth's seclusion, she might have thought that her answered prayer was only for her and Zechariah. She might have been tempted to create an over-protected life for this son, lest she somehow lose him. And indeed, in the end, she will lose John to the sword of Herod.

Mary's appearance at Elizabeth's doorstep reveals to her—and to you and me—that our life events are parts of a bigger plan than we know. Your prayers and my prayers are intertwined in ways we do not understand. We have a plan and a prayer life, and when things do not go as we want them to, we may weep and wonder and rethink and reinvent reasons our prayers aren't answered. We get anxious and fearful. We buy season tickets to the series called Suspense and spend our free time sitting in the dark, wondering what will happen next. God doesn't want that for you.

God calls us to live in mystery, sisters. Be not afraid.

Practical: Take Action

Elizabeth asks, "Why is this granted me, that the mother of my Lord should come to me?" (Luke 1:43). She does not know what the future holds for her little family. She does not know of John's place in the company of Jesus; that his baptism will unleash the Holy Spirit upon Jesus and that the entire script for the world will be rewritten to include words like forgiveness, redemption, mercy, and grace. She has no idea that her son will have a supporting role and is not the star, miraculous though his conception may be. Little does she know that the final scene of her only beloved son ends with a silver platter in Herod's court. She accepts the absolute mystery of life.

How can you not be afraid to live in mystery? One way you can embrace the unknown of today is to remember the faithfulness of God yesterday. The psalms are replete with wonderful examples of this:

> I will call to mind the deeds of the LORD;
> yea, I will remember thy wonders of old. (77:11)

> Remember the wonderful works that he has done,
> his miracles, and the judgments he uttered. (105:5)

Spend a few moments with these two psalms, noticing how the psalmist's laments and God's response are often paired together. Underline the call of the psalmist (77:8; 105:12, 13), and highlight the response of God (77:12-13; 105:14-15). God's response to the drama in the psalmist's life allows him to live in the mystery of the unknown as he trusts in God's faithfulness.

Now you can take some time to reflect on your life. Write down the events where you called in distress and the Lord answered in reply. Some of those times might have been "big things," like the end of a relationship or job you loved. But you might also recall some seemingly small ways in which God showed you his faithfulness. Did he help you through a time of sickness? Did someone extend grace to you when you felt you did not deserve it? Did a teacher give you encouragement when you were feeling disheartened? Can you see the faithfulness of God in the big things as well as the small?

As you spend time reflecting on God's faithfulness in your life, ask him for the gift of Elizabeth's faith for the situations you face today. Entrust each one to him, affirming your willingness to live in mystery.

The Serendipity of God

I wrote the last chapter during my first week of self-isolation due to the COVID-19 pandemic. Though a more chronological study would put the story of Elizabeth toward the beginning, I wanted the theme of mystery for my last chapter. The Bible seems to be a mysterious book to many of us.

Our lives and our futures have always been mystery, but the time we are in now seems more mysterious than most. Writing this book has taken on an unexpected significance. More now than ever, we need to encounter the Lord to gain strength, grace, and wisdom. We can do this by meeting the men and women he knew and loved and entering into their lives.

This is the serendipity of God. "Serendipity" is the gift of accidentally finding good amid everyday life. God continuously puts good things in our lives, and he delights when we find them.

I imagine the Lord smiling upon you as you dive into his word and make it your own. You will undoubtedly discover different insights than I have. You will make these women your friends and invite them over for coffee and scones, asking them questions I never thought to ask. This is the serendipity of God too.

Now, more than ever, we need to encounter the Lord to gain strength, grace, and wisdom. We can do this by meeting the men and women he knew and loved and entering into their lives. There are other women who have something to tell us from the depths of their souls and the experience of their world. They have names like Judith, Esther, Ruth, and Rahab. Perhaps that is another book for another time. The women whom we met in these chapters are women who knew Jesus and the power he had to change their lives. He has that power to change yours too.

This book was never about learning how to read the Bible; it is about deepening your relationship with the Lord. For the Lord is indeed inviting you to enter into the greatest mystery of all: his abiding, reckless, overpowering, *agape* love for you.

There is no wound the Lord is not eager to heal, no sin the Lord is not willing to forgive, no past the Lord is not ready to make perfect. The women in this book have shown us that. There is nothing to fear.

You own a Bible, and you know how to use it.

The Lord is waiting for you.

Roles in Judaism at the Time of Jesus

Since the Bible is a book written *by* a faith community *for* a faith community, there are some roles in the Jewish faith community that it can be helpful to understand as you dive into the word of God.

Pharisees

The Pharisees were somewhat like rabbis, the spiritual fathers of modern-day Judaism. Their name, Pharisees, means "separated ones," yet their focus was on the application of the Law to everyday Jewish life. Devout men with a heart for the Law and common people, they taught in the synagogues. They hoped for a return to the golden age of David and thus resisted Roman rule.

Theologically, the Pharisees accepted the entirety of the Sacred Scriptures, the *tanakh*. Because of the width and breadth of the *tanakh*, which includes the prophets and other extant writings, they believed in an afterlife, the coming of a Messiah who would also be King, and the presence of angels and spiritual beings.

Sadducees

The Sadducees were the party of the priests, aristocratic families, and merchants—the wealthier segments of the population. They tended to have good relations with the Roman rulers but were not as popular as the Pharisees among the Jewish people.

Theologically, the Sadducees emphasized man's free will and adhered strictly and exclusively to the *Torah*. They did not believe in angels, spirits, or the resurrection from the dead.

Sanhedrin

The Sanhedrin was the ruling council of the Jews. It consisted of seventy men—including Pharisees, Sadducees, and scribes—and was headed by the high priest.

Priests

The priests were of the tribe of Levi. They offered sacrifices on behalf of the people. The chief priest had the sole privilege of entering the Holy of Holies once a year, on the Day of Atonement, to make sin offerings for himself and for the people.

Scribes

The practical side of Judaism, these men copied the Sacred Scriptures for both the Sadducees and the Pharisees, and they worked alongside both. They were highly educated, well-respected, and well-trained professionals. They were known for their air of superiority and often suffered from pride.

Theologically, the importance of the *Torah* cannot be underestimated for these men. Obedience to the *Torah* was their hope for salvation.

Zealots

Banding together from disparate working-class families, zealots, more than most, would feel the sting of Roman rule and therefore desire to see it removed. While some zealots were peaceful—Jesus chose Simon the Zealot as a disciple—most tended toward mayhem, and some were not above murder. They worked against anything that kept the Romans in power.

People of the Land

The people of the land—normal, everyday Jewish men, women, and children—comprised 90 percent of the population in Jesus' time. They held a wide variety of occupations necessary for the flourishing of society. "Wealthy" would not be the adjective to describe them; dignified poverty was more the norm.

The people interacted with the Sadducees and Pharisees only when necessary, such as on matters of religious purity, demonic possession, and taxation. They were free to enter the Temple to pray, conduct business, solidify social ties, and have sacrifices offered.

Theologically, the people's beliefs mirrored those of the Pharisees.

Women

While men ruled in public community life, women ruled hearth and home. Their roles were to cook, clean, birth and raise children, and nurture the Jewish equivalent of the domestic church. The *Shabbat* prayers around the home table had the father at one end and the mother at the other.

Fathers arranged marriage for their daughters, sometime between the ages of fourteen and sixteen. A woman without a man to protect her was precariously perched in society. Virginity at the time of marriage was a given. A divorce could be exacted for any type of sexual misconduct.

In public, the roles of women were limited. Generally, women were to be modest in dress, could not witness in a court of law, and were to keep separate from men. The Temple had a designated prayer area just for women.

Exceptions to some of these norms occurred. A widow might engage in a small business, such as sewing or baking. Some unmarried women owned homes. Both Jesus and Paul had women friends who supported them financially in their ministries.

Notes

1. Fulton J. Sheen, *Three to Get Married* (New York, NY: Scepter Publishers, 2005), 107.
2. Pope St. John Paul II, *Letter to Women*, 12, http://www.vatican.va/content/john-paul-ii/en/letters/1995/documents/hf_jp-ii_let_29061995_women.html.
3. Pope St. John Paul II, *Letter to Women*, 4.
4. Pope St. John Paul II, *Letter to Women*, 10.
5. Footnote in *New Revised Standard Version,* Bible Gateway, https://www.biblegateway.com/passage/?search=John+8%3A2-11&version=NRSV.
5. Pope St. John Paul II, Homily for the Inauguration of His Pontificate, 5, October 22, 1978, http://www.vatican.va/content/john-paul-ii/en/homilies/1978/documents/hf_jp-ii_hom_19781022_inizio-pontificato.html.

About the Author

After being a stay-at-home mom for twenty years, Laura Stierman returned to academia and earned a B.A. and a master's degree in Theology (Sacred Scripture) at the University of St. Thomas and St. Paul Seminary and School of Divinity, respectively. She is a collector of wit, wisdom, and words, and dispenses them liberally when necessary. Her passion is her husband, their six children, and walking alongside women on a faith journey with the word of God.